Alan Bennett first appeared on the stage in 1960 as one of the authors and performers of the revue *Beyond the Fringe*. His stage plays include *Forty Years On*, *Getting On*, *Habeas Corpus*, *The Old Country* and *Enjoy*, and he has written many television plays, notably *A Day Out*, *Sunset Across the Bay*, *A Woman of No Importance* and the series of monologues *Talking Heads*. An adaptation of his television play *An Englishman Abroad* was paired with *A Question of Attribution* in the double bill *Single Spies*, first produced at the National Theatre in 1988. This was followed in 1990 by his adaptation of *The Wind in the Willows* and in 1991 by *The Madness of King George III*, both produced at the National Theatre. His stage version of *The Lady in the Van* was first seen in the West End in 1999.

by the same author

plays

PLAYS ONE
(*Forty Years On, Getting On, Habeas Corpus, Enjoy*)
PLAYS TWO
(*Kafka's Dick, The Insurance Man, The Old Country,
An Englishman Abroad, A Question of Attribution*)
THE LADY IN THE VAN
OFFICE SUITE
THE MADNESS OF GEORGE III
THE WIND IN THE WILLOWS

television plays
ME, I'M AFRAID OF VIRGINIA WOOLF
(*A Day Out, Sunset Across the Bay, A Visit from Miss Prothero,
Me, I'm Afraid of Virginia Woolf, Green Forms,
The Old Crowd, Afternoon Off*)
ROLLING HOME
(*One Fine Day, All Day on the Sands, Our Winnie,
Rolling Home, Marks, Say Something Happened,
Intensive Care*)
TALKING HEADS (BBC)

screenplays
A PRIVATE FUNCTION
PRICK UP YOUR EARS
THE MADNESS OF KING GEORGE

autobiography
THE LADY IN THE VAN (LRB)
WRITING HOME

ALAN BENNETT
Rolling Home

faber and faber

First published in this collection 2003
by Faber and Faber Limited
3 Queen Square London WC1N 3AU

Typeset by Country Setting, Kingsdown, Kent CT14 8ES
Printed in England by Mackays of Chatham plc, Chatham, Kent

One Fine Day and *All Day on the Sands* first published
in *The Writer in Disguise* by Faber and Faber Ltd in 1985
Copyright © Alan Bennett, 1985

Our Winnie, Rolling Home, Marks, Say Something Happened
and *Intensive Care* first published in *Objects of Affection*
by the BBC in 1982. Copyright © Forelake Ltd, 1982

Introduction by Alan Bennett, copyright © Forelake Ltd, 2003

This collection © Forelake Ltd, 2003

A CIP record for this book
is available from the British Library

ISBN 0–571–22043–6

2 4 6 8 10 9 7 5 3 1

CONTENTS

INTRODUCTION

A writer isn't the best person to analyse his or her work or to detect and detail its preoccupations. Still, I can see that in various stage and television plays – *The Insurance Man* (1985), *Kafka's Dick* (1986), *102 Boulevard Haussmann* (1991) and *The Lady in the Van* (1999) – I have been preoccupied with the writer's approach to his material.

Kafka said that to write is to do the work of the devil. I take this to mean that anyone who dispassionately observes the sufferings of his or her fellows rather than straightforwardly trying to alleviate such sufferings is collaborating in the pain. Kafka died in 1922, fairly early in the history of news photography, where the dilemma is more crucially posed and where the first instinct to assist often has to take second place to the professional need to depict. Still, it's the same dilemma as made Philip Roth, watching at his father's death bed, deplore his unseemly profession which, while sanctioning grief, at the same time required a degree of dispassionate observation, since this was material he would one day be able to use.

In the first play in this collection, *Our Winnie*, the photography student Liz sees the obliging but mentally handicapped Winnie as an ideal subject for her project and doesn't perceive there is a dilemma here. And nowadays 'I don't have a problem with that' is how she would describe it if she did.

In *Our Winnie* it's a straightforward case of exploitation, with the not very likeable student tricking Winnie's mother into letting her take photographs and, if excuse were necessary, presumably telling herself she is an artist or a professional and sheltering behind the privileges such designations are thought to confer.

What writers tell themselves I'm not sure (which is presumably why I keep writing about it).

The way the question most often poses itself, to me at any rate, is how fitting it is, how appropriate, how *excusable* to use one's own family background, parents, relatives and such as a resource, a memory bank from which to draw material. My parents were both shy people, so it's not simply a case of not presenting them in an unfavourable light, which I've never had reason to do; but presenting them at all would, if they knew of it, seem to them a violation. But that seems to me a part of the obligation of a writer and I take refuge in the remark of Flannery O'Connor, who said that anyone who has survived their childhood has enough information about life to last them the rest of their days. What is a writer to use but what comes to hand . . . though it's not always what *first* comes to hand, and certainly wasn't with me, as to begin with I saw nothing in my very ordinary life worth recording.

I was not alone in finding childhood dull and my parents not the stuff of literature. My Leeds contemporary Tony Harrison writes:

> Life . . . as I lived it, didn't seem to be the stuff that literature could be made of . . . We didn't have books in the house, so that my love of language and books always seemed to be a different thing from the life that I actually lived at home. Once I'd found a way of writing about that life, it all came back to me in the richest detail.

Like Harrison, it took me a while to realise that home was something I could write about, so my first plays were nothing to do with the north or with my family. It took me time to focus in on anything that had happened to me as a subject worth recording, so my first stage plays come out of reading and the imagination, with actual experience nowhere.

This question ought also to relate to the last play in this volume, *Intensive Care*. But I'm not sure that it does. Filmed in Airedale Hospital, near Keighley, in 1982, *Intensive Care* is the story of Hopkins, a shy, mild-mannered schoolteacher, easily mistakeable for me, whose father has had a heart attack and is in a coma. The son, whose relations with his father have never been wholly satisfactory, watches by his father's hospital bedside in the hope that his presence there when his father dies will make up for all his shortcomings and the ways he has failed his father in the past.

Always an awkward character, the father doesn't, of course, die to order but lingers and takes so long about going that when he actually does die Hopkins isn't at his bedside at all but tucked up with a night nurse on her afternoon off. He rushes to the bedside to find his father dead but with a smile on his face, a sign that in this, his last battle with his son, he has triumphed . . . and in injury time, too (*Injury Time* would have been another possible title).

The film was mostly shot in the same hospital in which my father died some eight years before. Like the father in the film, my father, too, died of a heart attack. And other similarities multiply. I myself played Hopkins in the film, though somewhat unwillingly. The house where my father was supposed to have lived was in Wortley, not far from where my father had once lived. The place names, names of characters and snatches of dialogue – particularly that in the mouth of Aunty Kitty (Thora Hird) – were all part of my own childhood.

But, all these similarities notwithstanding, I know that this is not my story and that my father in the film is not my father as he was. One is my father, the other (to put it pretentiously) is my child. And the central situation, a man's father dying while the son is having sex, was suggested by an episode in the life of someone quite remote from the Bennett family, namely Mahatma Gandhi.

The passage from Life to Art is neither as short or as direct as the reader or the viewer imagines, and seldom in my experience does anyone cross that border undisguised and with their belongings intact. And included in those belongings I would put age, gender, appearance, character . . . there is nothing that life does not surrender or art transform.

'I am not I,' wrote Evelyn Waugh of *Brideshead Revisited*, 'thou art not he or she; they are not they.'

All Day on the Sands is another visit to Morecambe. *Sunset Across the Bay* was to do with a retired couple living in Morecambe at the end of their lives; *All Day on the Sands*, while ostensibly set in the present, recalls some of the boarding houses where we used to stay in the forties. We seldom went in for full board, such as is on offer at the Miramar, instead taking our week's provisions in a cardboard box tied up with string, a receptacle which at the time I felt to be deeply embarrassing (I found it only too easy to find things to be embarrassed about all through my childhood). The landlady was generally regarded as an inimical figure by my parents, and the landlady's husband as a figure of fun, a music-hall view of the relationship that seemed not unrelated to reality and to the couple in the play.

In the dining room we always spoke in whispers, and even in the bedroom, too. What recalls those holidays vividly to me still is the smell of methylated spirits, used by my mother to dampen a small silver-cased pad on which she heated her curling tongs.

Boarding houses were cheerless places then, out of bounds to boarders except at meal times, so in Morecambe's often bitter weather we and dozens of families like us could be found tramping the streets or huddled in a shelter on the front. Given a fine day, we occasionally paddled or made sandcastles, though the sand at Morecambe, while superficially golden and attractive, at six inches down turns (a metaphor here) into mud.

Morecambe's enduring asset is the view, not that I ever recall noticing it as a boy. Across the sands of the bay one sees the Lakeland hills, snowcapped still in early spring when we filmed. It is a panorama that anywhere else in Europe would assure it of prosperity. But not here, and nowadays the town, once the 'Naples of the North', is even more run down than it was in 1978 when we filmed, the boarding houses taken over by students at the nearby University of Lancaster or the families of the unemployed and dispossessed living on benefit who these days tend to take refuge in English seaside resorts.

A liking for bare stages and empty sets partly explains the unrented office block which is the setting for *One Fine Day*. The play is a flight from clutter, both materially and emotionally, with Phillips, the discontented estate agent, taking up residence on the top floor of an empty tower block that he is trying unsuccessfully to lease. Looking for such a building briefly reconciled me to some of the unfeeling and mediocre architecture that was going up all over the country in the sixties and seventies.

When we found a suitable location it was in Wood Green, the building not particularly pleasing but, with or without Puccini, which plays pretty continuously through the film, I found it, particularly on summer evenings, a setting as compelling and evocative as Fountains Abbey had been in *A Day Out*.

Marks was slightly skewed in production because, though a naturalistic play, it was designed and shot in an almost experimental fashion with strong colours, jagged outlines and none of the understated working-class interiors I was used to and comfortable with. It was a deliberate experiment by the director and the designer, perhaps, though, reflecting a lack of confidence in the interest of the text. I went along with it, though I thought it confusing and unhelpful.

There was never any open disagreement as perhaps there should have been, but it is often the case that by the time a writer sees the projected design, often on the day of shooting itself, it's too late to do much about it, particularly if you're as timorous as I am. In my experience – and this applies to stage as well as television – authors are seldom given much credit for visual sense, the setting one carries in one's head when writing not being thought to be of much relevance when it comes to the design. To my mind, though, it's as pertinent as the words themselves.

Like *Me, I'm Afraid of Virginia Woolf, Marks* turns out in the final minutes to have been a gay play, though nobody noticed it at the time. It didn't exorcise my dislike for tattoos, which crop up several times in *Talking Heads*, generally as a class indicator or shorthand for someone being common. Never having liked these ornamental bruises, I still used to find their style of Fairground Primitive not unpleasing, with designs of flags and busty maidens a nice branch of folk art. Nowadays the style has changed to spiders and barbed wire, so even that compensation has gone.

The first series of *Talking Heads* ended with *A Cream Cracker under the Settee*, in which Thora Hird had a great success. At the time I had my doubts about the script, submitting it rather diffidently to Innes Lloyd, feeling that it covered old ground and that I'd said much of it already. Innes reassured me and of course it was well received and rightly taken as the peak of Thora's career. What I'd been worried about, though, was that several of the elements in *Cream Cracker* featured in an earlier play, *Say Something Happened*, in which a young social worker visits an oldish couple. As in *Cream Cracker* there turns out to be a child that is not spoken of, though whereas in *Cream Cracker* it is stillborn, in *Say Something Happened* it is retarded and living in a council home.

The sense of social isolation and the accident that lays Doris low in the monologue are here prefigured in the anxious warnings of the young social worker, played by Julie Walters. And though no one has ever compared the two plays, I did feel I was perhaps repeating myself. Not that a television audience minds that, or a theatrical audience either; as in other areas of human endeavour, it pays to repeat yourself: the public always like to know what they are getting.

Rolling Home, like *Intensive Care*, concerns an old man on the way out, the manner of both their exits shamingly similar. Just as in *Intensive Care* Mr Hopkins Sr. expires as his son is making out with the night nurse, so in *Rolling Home* it's while Donald the male nurse and his girlfriend are getting it together in the orderly room that Mr Wyman decides to go on his fatal walkabout. This was supposed to be taking place at night and the orderly room, since it was just off the ward, was meant to be the setting for a pretty discreet sort of coupling; no need to wake the patients after all. But Donald was played by David Threlfall, who, excellent though he was in other respects, had not been at the RSC for nothing. He managed to position his partner up against a metal hospital locker so that the latter stages of intercourse sounded like a troop of cavalry crossing an iron bridge, and not at all the stealthy knee-tremble I had had in mind.

We shot the film in a derelict hospital in Richmond, one of several such institutions I filmed in at this time (with another in *Intensive Care*), the availability and decrepitude of such locations I suppose saying something about what was happening to the NHS in the seventies and eighties.

As I am putting together this introduction comes the news of the death of Thora Hird at the age of ninety-one. Apart from her two *Talking Heads* monologues, these two volumes include all the plays on which we worked together. She did, of course, a great deal besides, but I count myself lucky that our paths crossed and that over twenty-five years she brought so much that I had written to vivid life.

Thora was a writer's dream, an actor who took the text seriously, never paraphrasing or diverging from it in the slightest degree. She said what you had written, trusting you as the author to know what you were doing, her reverence for the text nurtured in her early days watching and working on the plays of Harold Brighouse and Walter Greenwood. I am proud to have been of that company.

The last time I saw her it was to record a song from *Our Miss Gibbs*: 'I'm so silly when the moon comes out'. Though she was confined to a wheelchair, she still knew all the steps, her feet tap-ping away under the blanket as she sang the words and la-la'd the orchestral accompaniment. She had sung it first on stage at the Winter Gardens, Morecambe, when she was sixteen, and seventy-five years later she was still, as always, word-perfect.

Our Winnie

CAST AND CREDITS

WINNIE	Sheila Kelley
CORA	Elizabeth Spriggs
IDA	Constance Chapman
ERIC	Peter Lorenzelli
INTERVIEWER	Veronica Roberts
LIZ	Lesley Manville
FIRST ATTENDANT	Max Hafler
SECOND ATTENDANT	Jim Broadbent
IVY	Avril Elgar
CHARLES	Jimmy Yuill
UNDERTAKER	Jackie Shinn

Directed by	Malcolm Mowbray
Designed by	Stuart Walker
Music by	George Fenton

INT. SUBURBAN LIVING ROOM. DAY.

*A middle-aged girl in ankle socks, long coat and woollen gloves stands
expressionless in a room. Her shoes are too young for her. There is no
movement in her face. Her name is Winnie. She stands immobile long
enough for it to seem odd, then a woman in her sixties comes in: her
name is Cora. She is dressed, like Winnie, ready to go out. She opens
Winnie's coat and hitches the girl's skirt up.*

CORA Fasten your buttons. Come on. This button.

Winnie fastens it with great concentration.

This button.

Winnie fastens it.

This button.

Winnie fastens it.

And this button.

Winnie fastens it.

There. You can look really nice if you want to. It's done well
has this coat. (*Cora pulls the flaps out from the pockets.*) Your
hair'll want cutting in a bit.

She turns to go out of the room and Winnie sits down.

Don't sit down, Winnie. We're all ready. You don't sit down
when we're all ready. (*Cora puts on her hat and makes up her
face.*) We don't want to keep your Aunty Ida stood waiting. She
likes us there on the dot.

*Cora goes out. Winnie remains standing until Cora returns with
a bunch of carnations.*

If you're good you can carry the flowers.

They go out and we hear the outside door closed and locked.

Now – wait at the gate – Winnie.

*The empty room. The sideboard. A wedding photograph of Cora and
Frank, her husband. A later photograph of them with a baby.*

EXT. STREET. DAY.

*Cora and Winnie walk down various suburban avenues of nice semi-
detached houses.*

CORA Mind where you're treading.
Cora has to keep stopping for Winnie, who tends to stare in at gates.
Winnie! Keep up.
Winnie keeps up, and then draws ahead.
And don't take such big strides. Either racing on in front, else
lagging behind. You never get it right. I don't think you
concentrate.
*Winnie stops and stares at people, and Cora, catching her up, smiles
apologetically as she takes her hand and bustles her on.*
Watch where you're walking. This is where Doctor Handley
used to live. He delivered you. Flats now. His wife died. Right
refined woman. Always used to speak. Kept that garden lovely.
Somebody's chucked a mattress out. It's a right tip now.
*Winnie has started to pick some flowers, which she puts with the
carnations.*
See, Winnie! (*Cora takes the flowers Winnie has picked and throws
them away.*) Dogs go in there, and all sorts. Look at your nice
gloves. It's really disheartening. Keep in. They go mad round
this corner. Now then. You run on and see if you can see your
Aunty. Only think on, don't cross over.
Winnie runs on, as Cora calls after her:
And mind them carnations.

EXT. ERIC'S STREET. DAY.
*Winnie runs heavily down the street, and we see a woman waiting at
the corner, the same age as Cora but more spinsterly. This is Ida.*
*Winnie throws her arms round her with extravagant affection as Cora
catches them up.*
IDA I think she's losing her knickers.
CORA Oh. (*Cora undoes Winnie's coat and hoists them up.*) You
wouldn't lose your knickers if you were sensible and walked
properly. Stand up straight.
They walk down another street. More semi-detached houses.
IDA I thought you said your Eric was going to his Sub-Aqua.
He's in their garden.
CORA No.
IDA He is. He's just bobbed down.
*We see Winnie bent over the gate of a house, looking behind a hedge.
Cut to the garden of the house, where a young man is crouched
behind the hedge, being watched by Winnie.*

ERIC Go away. Go on. Sod off.

CORA'S VOICE Eric. Eric?

Eric stands up shamefacedly. He has been cutting the hedge.

ERIC Hello, Aunty.

CORA Have you not gone to your Sub-Aqua?

ERIC Christine just thought I could dispose of the hedge first. (*He looks apprehensively back at the house.*) I'm sorry I can't run you up there.

A car stands in the drive.

CORA Never heed. It's only a bus ride. We don't mind, do we, Ida?

IDA Where'd you do it?

ERIC What?

IDA Your Sub-Aqua.

ERIC Down at the Sports Centre.

CORA One of them torpedo things on your back?

ERIC We haven't actually got into the water yet. To date it's all been theory.

IDA Oh. I thought you'd have been a fully qualified frogman by now.

ERIC These things take time.

IDA Put paid to our little jaunts anyway. It was nice, the Capri. Breath of fresh air.

Cora ignores this.

CORA What will you do with it when you've got it, the Sub-Aqua?

ERIC Well . . . (*He is at a loss.*)

IDA Another string to his bow.

CORA There's all sorts gets chucked in the canal. Prams and what not. You could use it for that. You know, the environment.

IDA (*drily*) And folks are always drowning.

CORA Come away from that bell, Winnie.

Winnie has gone up to the front door and is twizzling the bell. The three of them go off down the street as Christine opens the door and looks crossly after them. Eric catches her eye and attacks the hedge again.

ANOTHER STREET. DAY.

IDA It wasn't as if we didn't chip in for the petrol. We were very scrupulous about that. We even put in a bit for wear and tear on the car. Well, we were no wear and tear, I'm sure. Then suddenly it's Sub-Aqua.

CORA It's Christine. She'll have put her spoke in.

IDA Sub-Aqua!

CORA He's young.

IDA Last year it was all Hang-Gliding. He went off that. It was just an excuse. He never liked taking us, that was the trouble. There was always some excuse. What was it the time he was supposed to be taking us out to Bolton Abbey? I know. That ox-roasting affair.

CORA It's her. She rules him.

IDA That's his fault.

CORA You don't know, Ida. You've never experienced it.

IDA What?

CORA Marriage.

Cora suddenly trips over Winnie, who has bent down to look at the pavement.

I'll give you such a clatter in a minute, young lady.

IDA Never mind, love. Come hold your aunty's hand.

Cora looks aggravated. The three of them walk on, Winnie happily holding Ida's hand.

CORA Young. Able to drive Heavy Goods Vehicles. You had the ball at your feet, Ida, if you'd only known.

IDA What's that supposed to mean?

CORA The war. You could have got a man then. It was all in the melting pot then.

IDA I didn't want a man.

CORA Well, you have to say that.

IDA I *didn't*. It's something you've never understood, you.

CORA Frank used to say: she'd have made a grand wife for somebody, would Ida. Frank liked you, Ida.

IDA I liked Frank.

CORA We had some grand times, the three of us. Real pals. Even after Winnie came along.

We see them approach a bus stop, where a young woman with a clipboard in hand steps out to meet them.

INTERVIEWER I wonder if you'd object to answering one or two questions. It's a survey.

IDA What sort of survey?

CORA A girl in Lewis's last week gave me a bit of experimental cheese. Got up as a Dutch girl.

INTERVIEWER It's a survey of public transport for the Corporation.

CORA Well, it wants surveying. You can be stood half an hour some times. (*to Ida*) Bonny little face. Mind you, we wouldn't ordinarily be using this bus. My nephew used to run us up.

IDA He's gone overboard for this Sub-Aqua.

CORA Shut up about Sub-Aqua. We live in the modern world. It's only a phase.

INTERVIEWER This is a random sample anyway. You don't have to be regular users.

CORA The eleven's better than the fourteen. The fourteen's very spasmodic.

Winnie is looking at a boy and girl, also waiting for the bus, who are leaning up against the wall, necking. Ida notices this, takes Winnie's hand and pulls her away.

INTERVIEWER Now, you're three?

CORA Two really. You'd better not put Winnie down. We never do. She's not right.

INTERVIEWER She's a passenger unit. She counts from a statistical point of view.

CORA She doesn't have a vote.

INTERVIEWER Now, you say you have access to a car?

CORA Yes.

IDA No, we don't. Not since he started doing this silly diving thing.

CORA It'll pass. The Sub-Aqua will pass. The Hang-Gliding passed. He's like that is our Eric. Very volatile. Put down 'occasionally'.

IDA Very occasionally.

CORA I wouldn't care, but Ida used to drive. She was a lorry driver. During the war. ATS. Heavy lorries. You wouldn't think so to look at her now.

IDA I couldn't do it now.

CORA You should have kept it up. A skill like that.

IDA I'd look a bit silly driving lorries now.

CORA She could dismantle an engine in thirty minutes flat.

IDA Well, the Queen was the same. She was in the ATS. I bet she hasn't kept it up.

CORA Yes, but you've more reason.
INTERVIEWER What's your starting point?
CORA How do you mean?
INTERVIEWER Where did your journey commence?
CORA Here. Amberley Road.
INTERVIEWER And what's your destination?
CORA Heywood. The cemetery.

EXT. CEMETERY GATES. DAY.
We see the three of them getting off a bus. The bus goes, and they walk towards some large gates. It is a cemetery-cum-crematorium on the outskirts of the city.
CORA All that's come in these last few years, surveys, asking folk what they think. Consultation's the keynote.
IDA I reckon nothing to it. It's these computers, wanting feeding. They install them, so they have got to give them something to do.
CORA No. I think they realise now. It's like these phone-in things. People matter. Now, Winnie, we don't want you running off. This is not a playground. See. (*She takes back the carnations from Winnie.*) Would you credit it? Twenty-five pence a bloom!
IDA Shocking.

INT. A ROOM IN THE CREMATORIUM OFFICES. DAY.
A public room, with seats round and in the centre a glass case in which is kept the Book of Remembrance. It is open and we see a list of names of those who have died on this particular day. A girl, a student named Liz, is looking at the book. She has a camera. Outside the room an Attendant waits, dressed in dark-blue uniform. Another Attendant sits at the side of the room, watching. The door opens and the Attendant comes in. Steps up to the case, unlocks it, lifts the lid, turns over a page of the book, closes the case and goes to the door again, where he stops and waits.
LIZ Is that what you usually do?
FIRST ATTENDANT Yes. I come in. I open the case. I turn the page over. I shut the case.
SECOND ATTENDANT Better turn it back. You turned it forward. It's been turned once today.
FIRST ATTENDANT All right, all right. (*He does this, rather crossly.*)
SECOND ATTENDANT He does it reverently. You do it reverently.

FIRST ATTENDANT Course I do it reverently. I'm not doing it reverently now because there's nobody here. If it's just me I come in and do it. I don't make a big performance of it. Only if there are any bereaved about I make it a bit more ceremonial. A bit more . . . military.

LIZ Try that then.

As he goes back to the door, Liz takes out her camera.
More . . . formally.
First Attendant comes in as before, but more smartly; gets to the case and stops.

FIRST ATTENDANT Do you want me to pause?

LIZ Would you pause?

FIRST ATTENDANT No, I mean besides that. Won't it blur?

SECOND ATTENDANT Blur? How do you mean blur? It won't *blur*. If you come in like Sebastian Coe it won't blur. It's one of these Japanese jobs. They don't blur. (*to Liz*) You should have asked me. I understand what you're on about.

FIRST ATTENDANT It's my day on.

SECOND ATTENDANT Yes, and any other day you'd be belly-aching.

FIRST ATTENDANT I'll start again.

SECOND ATTENDANT Blur!

The First Attendant comes in through the door and goes through the routine again. Liz snaps him at various points.

LIZ Would you do it again?

FIRST ATTENDANT Again? What am I doing wrong?

SECOND ATTENDANT Well, I don't mind doing it if you don't want to.

FIRST ATTENDANT No. I'm quite happy.

The First Attendant repeats the process, and is almost at the case when he is interrupted.

SECOND ATTENDANT And you'll have to turn the page *back* this time, remember.

The First Attendant stops, very cross.

FIRST ATTENDANT You've put me off. He's put me off.

He is furious with the Second Attendant, and Liz snaps him at this point.
Don't. That's not what I do. I thought you wanted an accurate picture. (*He goes out again, comes in, goes through the whole*

routine, gets to the Book of Remembrance and can't remember
whether to turn the page forwards or back.) Oh sod it.

LIZ Never mind. In any case the background's a bit dead. I really
want somebody else in the picture.

SECOND ATTENDANT Your own fault, love, for coming on a
Monday. Sundays you can't move. I'll go and get Ivy. She'll
welcome the excitement.

He goes out. The First Attendant looks at the Book of
Remembrance.

FIRST ATTENDANT This is what they call an illuminated
manuscript. The monks invented it. This . . . it's a work of art.

Liz looks sceptical. It's plainly not what she'd call a work of art.

EXT. CEMETERY. DAY.

Cora, Winnie and Ida are walking up a drive lined with laurels and
rhododendrons.

IDA Keep in, Winnie. We don't want running over.

CORA Well, if we were they wouldn't have far to take us.

They laugh, just as a hearse passes.

IDA We shouldn't be laughing.

CORA It's all done with split-second timing, this. Fast as one
comes out there's another ready to go in. No slump here.
They're not on short time, undertakers. This is where we cut
through.

IDA No, it is further up.

CORA Ida, he was my husband: we cut through here.

Ida shrugs and they cut through into the cemetery.

INT. OFFICE. CREMATORIUM. DAY.

Liz is looking out of the window and she sees Cora, Ida and Winnie go
by en route for Frank's grave. Liz is watching them when the Second
Attendant returns with Ivy, who is resentful and morose. Bereavement
is her bread and butter and some of it has obviously rubbed off.

FIRST ATTENDANT (*from outside*) Ready?

IVY Mondays is when I like to break the back of my correspon-
dence. Sad?

LIZ No. Just look.

IVY I would look sad, though, wouldn't I? Under the
circumstances.

SECOND ATTENDANT You might not have liked them.

IVY Who?

SECOND ATTENDANT The deceased.

IVY Why did I bother to come up, then?

FIRST ATTENDANT (*from outside*) Can we get on with it?

LIZ OK.

> *As the First Attendant marches in to turn the page, Ivy clutches her bosom in a parody of grief. Liz is not happy and takes no picture.*

LIZ I don't want you to feel anything.

IVY You're too young, you. You've never lost a loved one, probably.

LIZ Try talking.

IVY What about?

LIZ Chat.

IVY I wouldn't chat, would I, if I were bereaved? The bereaved don't chat.

SECOND ATTENDANT Some do. Some gab their heads off.

> *There is a strained pause.*

IVY I got the thumbs-down this morning.

> *First Attendant says nothing.*

I said I got the thumbs-down.

FIRST ATTENDANT Sorry, I thought you were just . . . chatting . . . you know, for her. For the camera.

IVY Well, if I were I wouldn't say that, would I? 'I got the thumbs-down this morning.' If someone tells you to chat you don't suddenly say 'I got the thumbs-down this morning' out of the blue. You say something like 'Haven't we been having some weather?' I'm carrying on a real conversation. I got the thumbs-down. Over the trouser suit.

SECOND ATTENDANT She's been trying to persuade them to let her come in a trouser suit.

IVY Let me tell her. I'm supposed to be the one who's supposed to be chatting.

SECOND ATTENDANT What'd he say?

IVY He said it smacked too much of leisure wear. Said, what was the matter with a plainish frock? I said I was fed up with plainish frocks. I said, if it's genuine grief it doesn't matter a toss what I wear.

FIRST ATTENDANT You didn't say that?

IVY I did. More or less.

SECOND ATTENDANT What did he say?

IVY Gave it the thumbs-down. Said we were treading a thin line.
How much longer is this going to go on? It's eroding my
morning is this.

She looks at her watch. Liz snaps her.

LIZ That was good.

FIRST ATTENDANT What did you do?

IVY Nothing.

SECOND ATTENDANT I'm getting it. I see what it is you're after.
It's life, isn't it? The genuine article. The camera cannot lie.

First Attendant glances through the open door.

FIRST ATTENDANT Ivy. You've got somebody waiting.

IVY Oh, blood and sand! (*She hurries out.*) They've come for
some ashes and I haven't done the documentation.

LIZ Sorry. Look, is there anywhere else we could go?

EXT. CEMETERY. DAY.

*Cora and Ida are walking along a path. We see Winnie, who is behind
them, run off among the graves.*

CORA I don't remember there being this path.

IDA We cut through too early.

CORA This is where I've always cut through.

IDA No. We cut through further up.

CORA You always have to be right, don't you?

IDA These are old graves.

CORA Some are and some aren't. They're that fast for room, they
put new ones amongst the old ones. They have to budge up.
Land, it's at a premium. He's next to somebody called
Eastlake. It's near a seat. (*She looks round.*) Where's Winnie?
Oh, hell and damnation! Winnie! Winnie! Winnie!

*They set off looking, and pass a student, Charles, sat on a
gravestone, drawing.*

Have you seen a big girl go past in a fawn coat?

CHARLES I'm sorry. I haven't been looking. I've been drawing.

CORA (*to Ida*) You go that way. (*She goes off, calling 'Winnie'.*)

IDA (*to the boy*) She's not right, you see. Winnie!

*Cora searches the cemetery. We see other students dotted about,
sketching. Cora sees Winnie stood among the graves.*

CORA Winnie! (*Calls.*) Ida! I've found her. She's here. (*She runs through the graves to Winnie.*) You've no business wandering off. Your mam's going to smack you.
Cora hits the back of Winnie's legs, as we see behind Winnie the name Eastlake. Winnie starts crying.
It's for your own good, love. You don't understand. There's all sorts of fellers about.
The student Charles is sitting not far away, and sees all this. Ida comes up as Winnie is still crying.
IDA Is she all right?
CORA Yes. (*She wipes Winnie's face.*)
IDA It's all right, love. Your mam and me are here. You're not lost.
CORA No. I gave her a smack.
Ida looks round.
IDA Well, she's found it. The grave.
Cora sees her husband's grave.
She knew where it was. And there's the seat.
Cora is mortified.
CORA Oh, Winnie. I'm sorry, love. Your mam's sorry. Give your mam a kiss. It was your mam's mistake. They've cut down that tree, that's what confused me. You can smack me if you want. Go on. Give your mam a smack.
She bends over, inviting Winnie to smack her bum. Winnie giggles, but doesn't.
IDA You're a clever girl, Winnie.
CORA (*pointing to the next grave*) Yes, you see: Eastlake.
IDA It was your mam's fault.
CORA All right, Ida. It was a genuine mistake.
She starts snipping at the grass on the grave with some household scissors she has brought.

EXT. A COLONNADE OUTSIDE THE CHAPEL. DAY.
The colonnade is lined with plaques, recording the names of the dead. There is the sound of singing from the nearby chapel as the Second Attendant lays out some wreaths. Liz hovers with her camera.
LIZ Talk, if you want.
SECOND ATTENDANT There's a service going on. (*Pause.*) They'll let you study aught now, students. Projects. We never went on projects. It's a hobby in my book, photography. It's pleasure.

The First Attendant arrives with more flowers. He is about to put his cigarette out but Liz, anxious to get a shot of him laying out the wreaths with a fag in his mouth, stops him.

LIZ No, don't put your cig out.

FIRST ATTENDANT No smoking in the chapel precincts. You'll have me sacked.

LIZ Nobody gets sacked these days. Do they? (*She is talking for the sake of talking, to distract attention while she is photographing them.*)

FIRST ATTENDANT It's not nice for the relatives.

LIZ Try leaning against the wall. No, keep the wreath.

SECOND ATTENDANT You'll have to be sharp. They'll be coming out in a minute or two.

LIZ They've only just gone in.

SECOND ATTENDANT It doesn't take long. It's only a formality after all.

Pause.

LIZ Talk – chat –

FIRST ATTENDANT Chat. Chat. We wouldn't chat here anyway, would we? The procedure is, we disembark the flowers, lay them out, then hop it. The bereaved don't like to see the staff.

LIZ Why's that? (*again, keeping them talking*)

FIRST ATTENDANT Why is it? Well, why is it, Harry?

SECOND ATTENDANT I don't know why. But I'm off.

FIRST ATTENDANT You were wanting to be in on it when she was taking me.

SECOND ATTENDANT Aye, but once you've had one or two goes it gets boring.

FIRST ATTENDANT Like everything else.

Liz, pissed off, waits as the doors of the chapel open and the mourners come out to look at the wreaths. Some bend over, looking at the names on the wreaths.

EXT. THE GRAVE.

Cora talks to Charles, who is sketching a statue on a grave.

CORA You've got her nose wrong. My husband could draw a bit. He was very good at horses. Horses are quite hard to draw, but they just happened to be his strong point. Can you draw horses?

CHARLES I haven't tried.

CORA Is that next term?

They both laugh, and he goes on drawing.

Will you get marked on it?

CHARLES Yes. And not so well either.

CORA Is that my fault? I'm not disturbing you?

CHARLES No.

EXT. COLONNADE. DAY.

Mourners. Liz quite discreetly snaps them. The undertaker notes this. He edges over to her without looking at her and says:

UNDERTAKER Are you official?

LIZ Yes.

UNDERTAKER In pink trousers? You never are. Out, lady, sharp. It's not a wedding. These are grief-stricken people.

LIZ I'm a student. We have got permission.

UNDERTAKER Not from me. Get lost.

Liz walks disconsolately away from the chapel, with her gear. She has a folded-up tripod as well as her camera.

EXT. CEMETERY. TAP. DAY.

Ida and Winnie are walking through the graves, Winnie with some dead flowers, Ida with a vase. Liz, Ida and Winnie are plainly on a collision course.

IDA Here's the bin. Throw them in. There's a clever girl.

Winnie holds the vase while Ida mans the tap. Together they fill the vase. Liz has spotted them and is desperately focusing her camera. Then she finds she is out of film.

LIZ Shit.

By the time she has got another roll in Ida and Winnie are slowly going back towards the grave.

EXT. CEMETERY. DAY.

Charles sketches while Cora chats.

CORA Your hair's nice and short. That's all come in again, short hair. I'd just got used to it being long, and now they've started with it short again. My forte was composition.

CHARLES Composition? Music?

17

CORA No! English. 'My holidays.' Composition was what it was
called. I used to have to stand up and read mine out many a
time. It's whether you have imagination or not. Course it's
all altered now. I was asking this little kiddy next door what she
liked best and she said Environmental Studies. I was staggered,
she's only nine. Then she talks about it – turns out she means
Nature Study. Here comes my party.
*Ida and Winnie are approaching, trailed at a distance by Liz,
camera at the ready. Winnie has been allowed to carry the vase,
which she is doing with exaggerated care. Cora takes it from her.*
That was a risk. It's her best coat.

IDA (*indulgently*) Well.

CORA Winnie, look at your new shoes. All plastered up. Oh, you
are a mucklump. Go and sit on that seat. Go on.
*Winnie goes and sits on the seat. Cora arranges the carnations in
the vase.*

IDA You expect too much of her.

CORA She knows more than you think.

IDA You ought to give her responsibility, not take it away. They
all say that nowadays.

CORA Who?

IDA Television.

CORA You don't know what it's like, day in, day out.

IDA She's company.

CORA She is and she isn't.

IDA It's a person. Someone there, choose what you say. You've
two plates to put out. Two cups. Someone to follow.

CORA You've no right to complain. It's what I say. You should
have got wed.
*Ida says nothing, just stands looking at the grave. Liz stands by
Charles, watching.*

CHARLES You can't. She's retarded. It's not fair.

LIZ It doesn't matter. Does it?
*Charles goes on drawing, looks furtively now and again as we see
Liz go up to Cora and Ida and start talking. Cut to the graveside.*

LIZ Can I take your photograph?

CORA What do you think?

IDA I take a terrible picture.

CORA We've been interviewed once today. Now we're going to have our picture taken. You students, I don't know.

IDA They get it all done for them now.

CORA We were born too soon, you and me, Ida. We should have been students.

LIZ I could be taking some now while you're talking.

CORA Oh no. I want to look nice.

Winnie has come over.

Winnie, what did I say? Go sit on that seat. Your shoes are all daubed up as it is. Your Aunty Ida and me are having our pictures taken.

LIZ Can't I take you all together?

CORA No. Winnie doesn't want her picture taking. She never has her picture taken. Her dad wouldn't have liked it.

IDA Nay, Cora, go on. Frank wouldn't have minded.

CORA Ida. She's my daughter.

Liz nearly snaps this exchange, but doesn't. Meanwhile Cora has taken out her powder compact and is just putting on a bit of make-up.

Just doll myself up a bit.

Ida waits as Cora puts on her make-up and Winnie stares straight at the camera. Liz takes a photograph.

You little monkey! I'm not ready. And I told you, I didn't want our Winnie's picture taking.

LIZ It wasn't a picture. I'm just focusing. You have to get the exposure right.

Charles hears most of this and looks fed up.

CORA We're not up in the mechanics of it. Anyway, Winnie, you've been told. Go and sit down.

Liz poses them, Ida on one side, Cora on the other. She takes out her tripod.

Oh, legs! Look, Ida, legs!

LIZ Talk.

They don't, but she takes one or two snaps. In the background Winnie sits on the seat, looking miserable.

CORA Easier for you than your friend.

LIZ What?

CORA Just clicking. Easier than your friend. Drawing. She's using a lot of pictures. Our Eric'll make a film last months.

IDA What's matter with Winnie? What is it, love?
    Winnie is crying.
    She wants her picture taking.
CORA No. I'm thinking of Frank.
IDA Go on, let her. Pretend. Don't click it.
    Cora is uncertain.
CORA If she promises.
LIZ All right.
IDA Put it on the legs. She'll want it on the legs, like ours. (*Ida does Winnie's hair and tidies her up.*) Sit up, love. That's it. Big smile for your Aunty Ida!
    Winnie smiles. Liz takes her photograph.

EXT. GRAVE. DAY.
Cora, Ida and Winnie have gone. Liz has her tripod set up. She has just taken a still photograph of the grave with its vase of carnations. Charles walks over as Liz packs her gear.
LIZ You'd draw her. Wouldn't you?
CHARLES It's not the same.
LIZ Why?
CHARLES I don't know.
LIZ You attend to people, that's all it is. You photograph people, you attend to them.
    It's not enough of an explanation for Charles, who senses also that Liz's photograph will be better than his drawing. He screws up the drawing and chucks it in a waste basket.
    Attention, these days, it's what people want.

INT. CORA'S HOME.
Tea is set out. Ida is looking at a photograph album as Cora comes in with the tea tray. There is a plate of cream cakes and Ida gives Winnie one, which she eats messily throughout this scene.
CORA That was taken in Leeds. We were just walking down Boar Lane and Frank says, 'Look out, this feller's taking our photograph.'
IDA You can just see him saying it. I can see him in Winnie so clear sometimes.
    Cora pours out some tea.
CORA We haven't done so bad today. We've been interviewed vis-à-vis the bus service. We've come into contact with the

younger generation and we've had our photographs taken. They're quite nice, some young people now, whatever you read in the papers. Those two were all right.

IDA Eric's two are demons. They look straight through you. You get the feeling you don't exist.

CORA (*looks at Winnie*) They don't know they're born, some of them. (*Cora goes back to the album.*) Redcar. Just after we were married. Cleethorpes. I won that doll. That's Winnie when she was little. That's you when you were little, Win. I don't think we can quite have known then. I think I realised first, only I didn't let on. Then I found he hadn't been letting on either. It turned out we both knew.

IDA I knew. He told me.

CORA He blamed himself. Putting it off till we got a house. We left it too late.

IDA You're not to know these things.

CORA We put her in for the *Evening Post* Bonny Babies competition. Sent her pictures in. I can't bear to think of it still. And people used to stop me with the pram and say what a grand baby.

Winnie's face is smeared with cream. Cora spits on her hanky and cleans her up.

Oh Win, you are a mucky trollop.

IDA Never mind. She's my friend, aren't you, love?

CORA Once we knew for certain, I didn't go out. Didn't go anywhere. I wouldn't take her out. Dad had it all to do. Dad and you. The housework. The shopping. Everything. It was long enough before I came round. Still, life has to go on, I suppose. Folks stare. They look at her and they don't realise. Then when they do realise, they look away. You don't want them to stare, and yet you don't want them to look away either. I don't know.

IDA It's a good job there's love.

INT. ART COLLEGE. EXHIBITION ROOM. DAY.
The camera tracks along a gallery, past various paintings and drawings of the cemetery done by the students, ending up on the photograph taken at the grave: Cora is putting on some lipstick, Ida stands looking into the distance, and Winnie stares directly into the

camera. It is a heartless photograph, but a striking one. It is also the one Liz said she had not taken, and it has won a prize. The final shot is of another photograph, the one Liz promised was only a pretend picture, of Winnie, sat on a seat, smiling vacantly.

All Day on the Sands

CAST AND CREDITS

All Day on the Sands was first transmitted by
London Weekend Television on 24 February 1979.
The cast included:

COLIN COOPER	Gary Carp
DAD	Alun Armstrong
MAM	Marjorie Yates
KEITH	Jonathan Coy
JO	Rosalind Wilson
MRS CATTLEY	Jane Freeman
FAY	Helene Palmer
MR CATTLEY	Ken Jones
MRS THORNTON	Lynne Carol
MR THORNTON	Clifford Kershaw
JENNIFER COOPER	Susan Hopkins
HARRY	Harry Markham
ALBERT	Albert Modley
MAN AT THE BOATING POOL	Bernard Atha
GRAHAM	Stephen Greenwood
DEREK'S FATHER	Bert Gaunt
DEREK	Lee Atkins
DEREK'S MOTHER	Liz Dawn
HILDA	Paula Tilbrook
LESLIE	Denis Bond

Produced by	Stephen Frears
Directed by	Giles Foster
Designed by	James Weatherup
Music by	George Fenton

PART ONE

EXT. TOWN. DAY.

A view across roofs, through chimney pots, television aerials and the backs of boarding houses towards the distant glitter of the sea. It is early morning.

INT. BOARDING HOUSE: TOP-FLOOR CORRIDOR. DAY.

Colin, a boy of twelve, closes a bedroom door. He walks along corridors, up and down two or three steps, round corners. A house that has been extended and converted. Through various fire doors until he comes to another corridor and knocks on a door.

COLIN *(a bit nervously)* Mam . . . Mam. Mam?

    Dad opens the door. A man in his late thirties. In pyjamas.

DAD What? What's the matter?

COLIN What time is it?

INT. BOARDING HOUSE: COOPERS' BEDROOM. DAY.

Colin gets past his father into the room, which is dark. His mother is asleep.

DAD What time do you think it is, coming in first thing? It's not seven o'clock yet.

COLIN Mam.

DAD You don't wake your mam. Your mam's on holiday.

COLIN Mam.

    Dad gets hold of Colin and pushes him out of the room.

MAM What is it? Colin?

DAD What do you want to be getting us up at this time for?

COLIN I've nothing to do.

DAD Well, we haven't anything for you to do.

MAM Read, love.

DAD Out.

INT. BOARDING HOUSE: TOP-FLOOR CORRIDOR. DAY.

Colin goes back down the corridor. As he is going, the bedroom door opens again and Dad puts his head out.

DAD And Colin. Don't wake our Jennifer.

INT. BOARDING HOUSE: COOPERS' BEDROOM. DAY.
Dad gets back into bed.
MAM (*turning over and going back to sleep*) What did he want?
DAD Shooting. Quarter to seven. (*Pause.*) Turn to me.
MAM No.

INT. BOARDING HOUSE: TOP-FLOOR CORRIDOR. DAY.
Colin goes back to his bedroom. More slowly. Fiddling with things.
Spitting carefully into a fire bucket. Looking out of odd windows. Very
quiet.

INT. BOARDING HOUSE: COLIN'S AND JENNIFER'S BEDROOM.
DAY.
Colin's unmade bed. A little girl asleep in another bed. She is between
nine and twelve. He wanders about the room. Looks at her. Maybe
plays with her teddy. He sits in front of the three-panel dressing-table
mirror and adjusts it carefully so that he can see a view of the back of
his head.
He opens the window and looks out at the back of the boarding house.
A version of the shot we saw at the start. A medley of roofs and
extensions. Below Colin's window a flat roof, about two storeys down.
There are a few pebbles in the room, obviously ones the little girl has
collected. He takes them and drops them one by one on to the roof
below, trying to hit an empty bottle which is standing there.
He finishes all the pebbles. He looks round the room. He picks up his
sister's sandal and looks round for some string.

INT. BOARDING HOUSE: JO'S AND KEITH'S BEDROOM. DAY.
A bedroom on the floor below. Jo and Keith, a young couple on their
honeymoon, are in bed. Keith is lying on his back. Jo half on top of him.
KEITH Jo.
JO What?
KEITH There's something banging on the window.
JO Who cares? (*Pause.*)
KEITH Where's my pyjama bottoms?
JO I don't know. You took them off.
KEITH *You* took them off. Where are they?

INT. BOARDING HOUSE: COLIN'S AND JENNIFER'S BEDROOM.
DAY.
*Cut to Colin upstairs dangling the sandal on a string out of the
window.*

INT. BOARDING HOUSE: JO'S AND KEITH'S BEDROOM. DAY.
Keith is looking out of the window.
KEITH Jo.
JO What?
KEITH It's a sandal.
JO Come on back to bed.
KEITH It's a sandal on a string.
JO We've not been married five minutes and all you're interested
in is sandals on strings.
KEITH Well, life has to go on. He's trying to knock over that
bottle. He's trying to knock that bottle over, Jo. Missed it that
time. He's having another go. Now he's in trouble.
JO If I'd wanted a running commentary I'd have married Eddie
Waring. Come back to bed.
KEITH He's lost his sandal. His sandal's come off.
We see the empty string going up past the window.
JO (*as Keith comes back to bed*) Flaming sandal. Come here.

INT. BOARDING HOUSE. COLIN'S AND JENNIFER'S BEDROOM. DAY.
*Cut to Colin in the bedroom upstairs, pulling in the string and looking
down at the sandal on the flat roof.*

INT. BOARDING HOUSE: KITCHEN. DAY.
*Mrs Cattley, the landlady, is cooking breakfast. She is busy putting
out delicate scalloped pieces of butter on to tiny plates. Two to a plate.
She puts three on one plate and with her fingers edges the extra one
on to another plate.*
MRS CATTLEY Two pats per person. Butter's bad for you anyway.
It's been proved in America. I'm doing them a favour.
Fay, an oldish waitress, is scraping toast.
FAY Marmalade. Where's the bloody marmalade?
Mrs Cattley holds a sauce bottle up to the light.
MRS CATTLEY Look at the level of that sauce! Only started
yesterday and it's gone down dramatically. I'm under no

compulsion to provide sauce. Lathering it on. It's not as if my cooking needed sauce.

FAY You want to make it available on request. 'Sauce available on request.' That might bring them to a sense of responsibility.

MRS CATTLEY I wouldn't care but they go at the salt and pepper like mad things. You'd think they'd never seen a cruet in their lives. Pigs. Pigs' tea. Pigs' toast. Pigs' marmalade.

Two tones on the tannoy herald an announcement and a look of long-suffering contempt comes over Mrs Cattley's face as we hear her husband begin his announcement.

MR CATTLEY (*over tannoy*) Hi, all you leisure-lovers. Eight o'clock, the temperature is 52 degrees and it's fair to cloudy in midtown Morecambe. This is your Miramar host, Percy Cattley, saying hello again and welcome to another fun-packed day.

INT. BOARDING HOUSE: HALL. DAY.

Cut to the hall where Mr Cattley has a little cubbyhole under the stairs from which he broadcasts.

MR CATTLEY (*continuing*) The service of breakfast will shortly be commencing in the Portofino Room. Top of this morning's menu are kippers, fresh in from Fleetwood, the best Poulton le Fylde can do in the way of bacon plus free-range eggs and your choice of starters: orange juice, pineapple juice, tomato juice, grapefruit segments, or melon balls.

In the doorway we see Colin looking up inside the shaft of the dumb waiter.

Leave that alone, unless you want decapitating.

Colin watches him expressionlessly, which makes Mr Cattley slightly self-conscious.

May I remind you that breakfast is from eight until nine-thirty so Mrs Cattley and I look forward to seeing you shortly in the Portofino Room.

MRS CATTLEY (*coming through with some dishes*) And no latecomers.

MR CATTLEY So rush, rush, rush to the Portofino Room.

The two tones go, indicating the end of transmission.

INT. BOARDING HOUSE: PORTOFINO ROOM. DAY.

Empty. Not all the tables are set. The place is plainly not full. Colin sits at a table for four. Fay ignores him.

FAY I'm not serving you, young man. There's four of you. You'd
better wait till you've got a full complement. Yes?
*She waits to take the order of an older couple who have come in and
sat down at the next table. Conscious of her presence, the couple
communicate in an undertone.*
MRS THORNTON I thought I might try the kippers this morning
but I don't know whether I dare. They have a tendency to
repeat. What do you think?
MR THORNTON If you want them, have them.
MRS THORNTON I don't know whether I do.
MR THORNTON Well, have bacon.
MRS THORNTON Shall I?
MR THORNTON She's waiting.
MRS THORNTON What are you having?
MR THORNTON Bacon. She'll have bacon. And I'll have bacon too.
Fay goes away.
MRS THORNTON I wanted kippers.
FAY (*out of vision, as Colin gets up and goes out*) Two bacon.

INT. BOARDING HOUSE: UPSTAIRS CORRIDOR. DAY.
*The corridor leading to Colin's and Jennifer's room. Piped music. Mam
walking with Jennifer, one shoe on, one off.*
MAM Do you remember taking it off?
JENNIFER Yes.
MAM Well, it must be there somewhere.

INT. BOARDING HOUSE: COLIN'S AND JENNIFER'S BEDROOM.
DAY.
*Mam looks under the bed. In the empty echoing drawers of the dressing
table. In the vast wardrobe.*
MAM You'd better put your best on.
JENNIFER They hurt.
MAM That's your look-out.
JENNIFER My feet get hot.
MAM I'll clatter you if you're not careful. Where is it?
*She looks in the bottom of the wardrobe. Through the open door we
hear the sound of the tannoy . . .*
MR CATTLEY (*over the tannoy*) . . . the finest Fleetwood kippers,
plus free-range eggs and your choice of starters: orange juice,

grapefruit juice, tomato juice, grapefruit segments or melon balls. Service of breakfast in the Portofino Room will be terminating in approximately ten minutes' time and I am asked to say that staff shortages and the prevailing economic climate make it impossible to serve latecomers.

MAM Where do you think we find money for new sandals now we've naught coming in? It doesn't run to new sandals, Social Security.

INT. BOARDING HOUSE: STAIRS/LANDING. DAY
Dad waiting at the head of the stairs.
DAD Lil! Lil!
MAM (*out of vision*) Coming.

INT. BOARDING HOUSE: STAIRS/HALL. DAY.
Mam, Dad, Colin and Jennifer are going downstairs.
MAM And think on, don't let on.
JENNIFER What?
MAM You know. About your dad. And Colin, you neither.

INT. BOARDING HOUSE: PORTOFINO ROOM. DAY.
One or two more guests have appeared. The Thorntons are still there at the next table to Mam and Dad (whose name is Cooper). A youngish man and somewhat older woman are at another table. The Coopers have sat down when Keith and Jo, the honeymoon couple, get in at the last minute, nearly knocking down Mrs Cattley, who is coming out as they are going in.

INT. BOARDING HOUSE: KITCHEN. DAY.
MRS CATTLEY It always has to be the last minute. I could be serving breakfast while twelve o'clock and they'd still be poling in at two minutes to.
MR CATTLEY They're honeymooners, Denise. I like to think that at the Miramar we give them a bit of elbow room.
MRS CATTLEY Oh, is that what it's called – elbow room? Sex till a hair's breadth of nine-thirty and it's elbow room. Well listen, Alvar Liddell, I'm the one that wants elbow room.

INT. BOARDING HOUSE: PORTOFINO ROOM. DAY.

Fay is taking the Coopers' order.

FAY Segments. Segments. Segments. I've got three segments.

COLIN (*whispering to his mam*) I can't have flakes and segments?

MAM No. He can't have flakes and segments?

FAY No. That's your choice of starters.

COLIN (*whispering to his mam*) What if I didn't have scrambled egg?

MAM What if he didn't have scrambled egg?

FAY I can't be doing permutations on it. Flakes or segments?

COLIN Flakes.

MAM (*whispering*) Jennifer'll give you some of her flakes.

JENNIFER I won't.

MAM You've lost your sandal, miss. You'll do as you're told.

JENNIFER Dad.

DAD Do as you're told.

MAM You two, you do show us up.

MR THORNTON Grand day again.

DAD Ay.

MR THORNTON Mind you, May, it generally is nice. They've proved that statistically. Jodrell Bank.

MRS THORNTON But it's funny, I was saying to Edgar, we always seem to hit on a good week weatherwise. We did last year, didn't we, Edgar? Never saw a drop of rain.

MR THORNTON We always try and get in before the crowds. There's not much going off but we like that.

MRS THORNTON We like that. July, it gets a bit common. You get all sorts nowadays.

MAM Oh, yes. Jennifer, sit still. And put your feet under the table. She's lost her shoe.

MR THORNTON Cinderella.

MAM Last year we went to Minorca, only we thought we'd have a change this year.

MRS THORNTON Oh. Majorca.

MAM Minorca. It's the adjacent island.

MR THORNTON Frankly, I wouldn't thank you for Majorca. Minorca. Any of those places. I always say to Hetty when we go out on a morning, 'Breathe in, Hetty. You'll not find finer air in the whole of the Western Hemisphere.'

MRS THORNTON And he knows. He was in Malaya during the
Emergency.
Mam is watching the older woman, Hilda, and the younger man,
Leslie. They look happy. This is his special marmalade.
No (*mouthing*) sugar.

MAM Jack could do with slimming. I'm always on to Jack to slim.

MRS THORNTON No. He's (*mouthing*) diabetic. He can be going
along right as rain. The next minute he's in a coma. I watch
him like a hawk. Whereas ten years ago he would have been a
dead man, he now has his special marmalade and he's
champion. It's what I say, you learn to accommodate.

MAM You have to.

MRS THORNTON It's like my sister-in-law. She's only got half
a stomach yet she leads a perfectly normal life.

MAM Where's that?

MRS THORNTON Batley.
Mam watches the honeymooners.

MAM Do you think they're married?

DAD Which?

MAM Them two.

DAD I don't know. Ask them. Why?

MAM They're only young if they are. Could we have a drop more
hot water?

MR THORNTON What's on the agenda for today?

MAM I don't think we'll go far.

FAY (*out of vision, shouting down the hatch*) More hot water now.

MR THORNTON We had quite a hectic day at Heysham yesterday so we're not going to overdo it. Hetty wants to see if she
can pick out a frock and I've some business to transact at
the Post Office. We'll probably stagger down to the beach
later on.

MAM I don't think we'll get much further than the sands today.

MR THORNTON Well, that's what it's all about, isn't it? Giving
yourself time to unwind. What's your line of thing?
There is a perceptible moment of awkwardness.

DAD Well, I'm . . .

MAM He works at this engineering firm in Leeds. Leeds.
Engineering.

DAD I'm a supervisor. Components.

MR THORNTON Oh, *components*. They're the thing these days. I'm self-employed.

MRS THORNTON We have a little gents' outfitters. He goes in, but he's more or less semi-retired now, aren't you, Edgar?

MAM One of these old family firms. He's been very happy there. They think the world of him.

MRS THORNTON Well, they're the best, aren't they? There's that much redundancy now.

MR THORNTON Well, Alice, there is and there isn't.

MRS THORNTON Yes, I think there's work if you really scout around.

MAM Oh yes, I'm sure there is.

MR THORNTON A lot of these fellers, if they can get themselves as far as the labour exchange they reckon they've done a week's work.

DAD That's right.

MRS THORNTON Shocking.

The children say nothing. At the honeymooners' table . . .

JO What do you want to do today?

KEITH I don't know. What do you want to do?

JO I don't know. We'll do what you want to do.

KEITH I want to do what you want to do.

JO I don't want to do anything in particular. You know. I just want to be together.

KEITH But we have to be together doing something. Would you like to go to Fleetwood?

INT. BOARDING HOUSE: HALL. DAY.
The Coopers have come out of the Portofino Room. Mrs Cattley is waiting.

MRS CATTLEY Mrs Cooper. No bare feet in the Portofino Room, if you don't mind.

MAM She's lost her shoe.

MRS CATTLEY It's a rule of the house. We have to draw the line or else they'll be waltzing in in bikinis.

The Thorntons have overheard this.

MAM (*to Jennifer*) You don't half show us up.

MR CATTLEY (*into tannoy, voice under preceding dialogue*) Our dish of the day this evening will be duck à l'orange: fresh Aylesbury duckling in a tangy orange sauce together with crisp Norfolk peas and duchesse potatoes. There'll be another chance to sample Mrs Cattley's famous trifle, followed by After Eight mints and a choice of beverages.

MRS THORNTON This regime suits us. We generally have our main meal at night.

MR CATTLEY (*into tannoy*) Those patrons who have ordered lunch-boxes will find them waiting for them now in the Marbella Lounge. Weight-watchers are recommended to try our slimline lunch pack specially selected to form part of your calorie-controlled diet. May I also remind patrons that Messrs Heaps run luxury coach trips every evening to specially selected beauty spots. Venue for this evening's trip is Newby Bridge, Mecca for the discerning sightseer. Patrons are advised to book early to avoid disappointment.

INT. BOARDING HOUSE: KITCHEN. DAY.
Mrs Cattley is up to her elbows in greasy water, trying to unblock the sink. Fay is piling up the dirty plates. Over the tannoy comes the end of Mr Cattley's morning transmission.

MR CATTLEY (*voice over*) Patrons are particularly requested to return their lunch-boxes together with their plastic utensils. There is a receptacle for returned utensils in the vestibule. Have a good day now.

MRS CATTLEY When Emperor Rosko comes off the air tell him the sink's blocked.

INT. BOARDING HOUSE: MAM'S AND DAD'S BEDROOM. DAY.
MAM Has she come out? Jennifer. Go watch to see when she comes out. You'd think they could run to more than one toilet per floor, wouldn't you? It's with them being so hot on fire regulations. They spend all the money on that and toilets have to take a back seat. Have you looked for that shoe?

COLIN I can't find it.

DAD You'd better find it. I'm not budgeting for new shoes.

INT. BOARDING HOUSE: CORRIDOR. DAY.
Jennifer is waiting smack outside the WC. Door opens. A woman comes out.

JENNIFER (*calling*) Mam! She's out.

INT. BOARDING HOUSE: MAM'S AND DAD'S BEDROOM. DAY.
MAM I'll wait a minute. I never like to see who's been in before
  me. (*She waits.*)

INT. BOARDING HOUSE: CORRIDOR. DAY.
JENNIFER Somebody else went in.
MAM Well, go and look for your sandal, go on.

INT. BOARDING HOUSE: COLIN'S AND JENNIFER'S ROOM. DAY.
JENNIFER You look.
COLIN No.
JENNIFER Why?
COLIN What's the use?
JENNIFER I don't like these shoes. I wish we were in Minorca.
  I never wore shoes.

INT. BOARDING HOUSE: PORTOFINO ROOM. DAY.
*Fay is sitting at a table in the window in the now empty dining room
having her breakfast. Through the window we see the Thorntons going
out, followed by the Coopers.*
FAY Glued to that flaming microphone. There's I don't know
  what swilling around in that sink and all he does is broadcast.
  Over and out. Well, I'm over and out after thirty-five breakfasts
  and nineteen early morning teas. What about my varicose
  veins? He wants to broadcast them. Pete sodding Murray. I'm
  jiggered . . .
Mr Cattley passes and overhears her chuntering.
MR CATTLEY Well, why do you do it, then, Fay? We're not forcing
  you. (*He goes upstairs.*)
FAY Why? Because I'm saving up for some decent teeth. Some
  proper, private teeth. Some teeth that fit. I want teeth I can eat
  toast with. (*Tries to eat a slice of toast.*) Nay, I can't eat this
  toast.

EXT. STREET. DAY.
The Coopers and the Thorntons walking towards the promenade.
MRS THORNTON We like Morecambe. Blackpool's a bit on the
  common side. Morecambe's more refined. Only they're trying
  to spoil it here now. Discos. Miss World.

MAM It's nice for the kiddies.

MRS THORNTON Yes, only it's all kiddies now, isn't it?

MR THORNTON (*talking to Dad*) We debated whether or not to bring the car but parking's the problem. Everywhere's the same these days. It's not worth running a car. Are you motorised?

DAD We've just got the mini but the suspension was a bit dodgy so I thought we wouldn't risk it.

MR THORNTON I know the feeling. When you've got a couple of hours to spare I'll tell you the saga of my clutch.

DAD Oh ay.

EXT. PROMENADE. DAY.

Mr and Mrs Thornton and the Coopers going along the promenade.

MRS THORNTON There's just that nice breeze.

MR THORNTON We can't do with it too hot, can we, Hetty?

MRS THORNTON No, Edgar can't do with it too hot and I can't either.

MR THORNTON That's another reason why we steer clear of abroad. It does tend to be sweltering.

MRS THORNTON Then there's the language problem. I have to think of him, you see. Say he went into a coma. I couldn't explain that in Spanish.

MR THORNTON No, it's overrated is abroad.

MRS THORNTON And he knows. He was in Malaya.

MR THORNTON If I had to choose between Morecambe and Kuala Lumpur I'd plump for Morecambe any day. Just look at that! (*Stops to survey the view across the bay.*) You wouldn't find that in Kuala Lumpur! Torremolinos neither.

EXT. BEACH. DAY.

The Coopers have got two deckchairs and are walking along the sands.

DAD What's matter with here?

MAM No. (*She walks on.*)

DAD Why? Why?

MAM What do you think them seagulls are? That's a sewage pipe.
  She indicates a spot five hundred yards out in the bay.

DAD There?

MAM It washes in. It has to go somewhere.

DAD Well, be sharp or else we'll be in Grange. Here?
JENNIFER Mam. I'm cold. I'm cold, Mam.
MAM Well, all right, then.
DAD Right. Your mam's approved the site.
They set up deckchairs and Jennifer begins to put her costume on.
What're you putting your costume on for if you're cold?
JENNIFER It's the seaside.
MAM Aren't you going to put your trunks on?
Colin shakes his head.
Nobody's looking.
COLIN I don't want to, anyway.

EXT. BEACH. DAY.
Jennifer has a child's book about seashore life.
JENNIFER There's none of these here, Dad.
DAD What?
JENNIFER There's none of these here.
Dad looks at her book.
DAD There's shells. What more do you want?
JENNIFER Starfish.
DAD There aren't starfish at Morecambe. There aren't starfish anywhere much now.
JENNIFER Crabs?
DAD There'll be some crabs. Only they'll be fiddling little 'uns. You can't expect MacFisheries' crabs. Ask Colin to show you.
JENNIFER He won't.
DAD Play with your bucket and spade, then. Your mam'll take you to look later on. (*Picks up the book.*) Marine Life. Crabs. Lobsters. Look at that! Sea-horses. I've never seen a sea-horse in my life. And starfish. It's not fair. Putting ideas into their heads. It makes them disappointed. Even the shells. There's none of them shells, is there?
MAM You can buy them in shops. Proper shells. You can't expect to find them just lying around.

EXT. BEACH. DAY.
DAD The tides are controlled by the moon. Did you know that?
COLIN Yes.
DAD How? You didn't.

COLIN I did. We did it at school.

DAD You didn't, did you?

MAM Didn't what?

DAD Know the moon controls the tides.

MAM Well, it's not out.

DAD What do you mean?

MAM The moon. It's not out. So how can it control them?

DAD It doesn't have to be out, does it, Colin? Your mam thinks it has to be out first. It's up there somewhere, and it controls the tides.

MAM Do you mean if it's a full moon the tide's up and if it's not it's only halfway?
Pause.

DAD I think it's more complicated than that. Do you know, Colin?

COLIN No.

DAD I thought you said you'd done it at school.
Pause.

MAM Anyway, it doesn't do much of a job here, does it?

DAD What?

MAM The moon. Tide's never in. Slipping, moon. Bad as the Corporation.
Colin laughs.

DAD Oh ay, that's right. Don't believe me. You make them laugh at me, don't you? Well I'm not going to say aught. Their thick father. (*Pause.*) Their thick, unemployed father. You believe me, don't you, Jennifer?

JENNIFER What?

DAD About the moon.

JENNIFER Wasn't listening. I'm cold.

EXT. BEACH. DAY.

COLIN I'm bored. (*Pause.*) I'm bored, Dad. (*Pause.*) Dad. I'm bored.

DAD You're twelve years old.

COLIN I am.

DAD It's grown-ups that are bored. You're having the time of your life.

COLIN I'm bored.

DAD Well, if you're bored now, you'll be more bored when you're grown up. It gets more boring as you go on.

MAM You bore me.

COLIN You bore me.

Dad clouts him.

MAM Jack!

DAD I don't care. Saying that. We come away on holiday and then he's the cheek to say he's bored.

Colin goes off at this point.

MAM I am getting old arms. My arms. Getting to look right old.

DAD Why single out your arms?

MAM Well, I notice you haven't got into your costume.

DAD Why should I? Who is there to impress?

MAM Impress! With that belly?

DAD I impressed you once.

MAM Ay. You did. You did that. Funny, we've never been to Filey since.

JENNIFER I'm cold.

MAM If you say you're cold once more, young lady, I'll think of something to warm you up.

DAD Come here, love.

Jennifer sits on his knee.

EXT. BEACH. DAY.

MAM I don't like watching TV in a roomful of folk. (*Pause.*) Do you?

DAD Do I what?

MAM Like watching with people you don't know.

DAD It's all right. *Match of the Day.*

MAM It's not the same as watching it on our own. I'd rather go to the proper pictures. I hate being sat there with a jorum of folks not knowing what they're like, wondering what they're all thinking. (*Pause.*) Plays. I can't watch plays among strangers. They have to be people I know. Preferably the immediate family. (*Pause.*) You can't talk to it.

DAD What?

MAM The TV. I like to talk to it.

DAD Don't start talking to it up there or they'll think you're barmy.

MAM Everybody talks to it. Acts daft. If they're on their own, and they think nobody's watching. I do.

DAD I don't.

Pause.

MAM You're not your own master. Where Dugdales stayed, the Clarendon, that has TV in every bedroom. Shower and TV. 'Private hotel.' It's not a proper private hotel. It's not even that clean. (*Pause.*) That pillow had hairs on it.

DAD My hairs.

MAM They weren't your hairs. I know your hairs. I should know your hairs by now. Your hairs aren't like that. They were somebody else's hairs. Little curly ones. I found another one there this morning.

DAD They won't kill you. The army, we never even had pillow-cases. Hairs.

Pause.

MAM I think it's that that's stopping me sleeping.

DAD What?

MAM Them little hairs. I've not had a proper night since we came. Let alone anything else.

DAD Well, whose fault is that?

MAM No. I mean the other. At home I always go like clockwork.

DAD You said the same at Marbella.

MAM No, I was the other way at Marbella.

DAD It's the water.

MAM It's partly the water. But I'm not struck on that toilet. I don't like them low suites.

DAD Go to one of the other ones.

MAM It's half a mile. They're like everything else these days, designed for what it looks like. Whereas we're not. We're not designed for what it looks like, are we?

DAD What?

MAM Bottoms!

DAD Lil! I don't know. We come away on holiday and you get right unsavoury. Toilets. Read the paper.

EXT. BEACH. DAY.

JENNIFER Dad. Dad.

MAM Jennifer.

JENNIFER Dad.

DAD What?

JENNIFER Do you like it here?

MAM Jennifer.

DAD Why?

JENNIFER It's cold. The sea's not blue. It's blue abroad.

MAM I've told you not to talk about abroad. Your father doesn't want to know about abroad. You're lucky to have been abroad. We'd never been abroad at your age. Abroad. We only came on this holiday for you.

DAD I don't know why we did. When you reckon it all up there's not much difference in price. That place isn't cheap for what you get. And I'm always hungry.

MAM You pay for him on that radio, that's what you pay for. (*Pause.*) Do you think that couple at the little table are married?

DAD Not if he's any sense.

EXT. SEASHORE. DAY.

Colin wanders down through the people sitting on the sands, out into the bay, trying to walk to the edge of the sea. Miles and miles of empty sand. The beach is very small and distant behind him. The very faint sound of the beach. Finally he reaches the edge of the sea. But he isn't sure whether it really is the edge, it's so gradual and undramatic. He is called back by shouts of 'Colin!'

EXT. BEACH. DAY.

Dad gets out the plastic boxes they have brought from the boarding house. 'Your Eats' is written on the top of the boxes.

DAD 'Your Eats.' Here, Colin, 'Your Eats.' 'Your Eats.'

MAM What's yours?

DAD Ham, I think.

MAM Ham.

DAD There's a broad bean in mine. D'you ever hear of a sandwich with a broad bean in it? What sort of a sandwich is that? And all these doll's knives and forks. If they spent a bit more on the food and a bit less on what you're supposed to eat it with. Look, individual salt and peppers. (*He flings them into the sand.*)

43

COLIN Litter. Dad. Litter. Mrs Monkman at school says litter's a crime. Mrs Monkman says people ought to be put in prison for dropping litter.

Colin goes and picks up the salt and pepper and puts them back in the box.

DAD Now you've gone and got all sand in the box, you silly little sod. What does Mrs Monkman say about that?

MAM Don't call Colin a little sod. Calling your own son a sod.

DAD He's my son. I call him what I want.

MAM It's all to do with airlines. That's what's done all that. It all has to be like airlines now. All this plastic cutlery. Little salt and pepper. It's pretend we're on an aeroplane.

JENNIFER I wish we were on an aeroplane.

DAD Shut up.

MAM Yes. You lost your sandal. Like trains. They have this voice telling you how fast you're going and there are buffet-car facilities available on this train. It's all splother. All of a sudden everything has to be such a performance. 'Your Eats.' And one scrutty little apple.

DAD Ay. If this is the ordinary one God knows what the weight-watchers get. I've finished mine. Look out. The vultures are gathering. (*He throws stuff to the seagulls.*)

COLIN Mam.

MAM What?

COLIN I want something hot. Can I have something hot?

DAD Eat them. We've paid for them.

COLIN Can I not have a pizza?

DAD No, you can't have a pizza.

COLIN Mam.

DAD I said no. You can't have a pizza.

MAM Anyway, where can you get a pizza?

COLIN We passed a place. On the front.

DAD And who's going to pay for it? It's want, want, want. We've got nothing coming in now, you know. You still think your dad's made of money. They don't give you hand-outs for pizzas.

JENNIFER I don't. I don't want a pizza.

COLIN You lost your sandal.

Mam gives him some money from her purse.

MAM Here, love.
    Colin goes.
    Well, it's their holidays. Pizzas. We never had pizzas, did we?
    Still, it's only cheese on toast. It's Welsh rarebit really. Except
    pizzas are round and Welsh rarebit's square. All that's new as
    well.
    Pause. Dad stares gloomily out to sea.
    What's matter?
DAD Nowt.
MAM You'll find something when we get back. It's on the turn
    now. They all say that. It's in the paper.
    *She settles down with the paper, occasionally reading out headlines
    as Dad dozes off.*
    'Blackburn gripped by bread hysteria.'
    'Pensioner cleared of teacake theft.'
    'Pope braves drizzle.'

EXT. BEACH. DAY.
*Much of the conversation between Mam and Dad in the deckchairs
is quite pausey, often because he is half-asleep. This exchange is done
very slowly with lots of gaps.*
MAM Dad.
DAD What?
MAM Was it tomato, them sandwiches we had at Rhyl?
DAD When?
MAM We had some right nice sandwiches once. Just after we
    were married. At Rhyl. Were they tomato?
DAD I don't know.
MAM I don't know either.

PART TWO

EXT. BEACH. DAY.

A stone pier on the front. Men fishing. A coin-in-the-slot telescope.

Two old men are sitting on a seat in the sun.

HARRY I was going to have my hair cut this week. I should have gone last week. It'll have to wait while next week now, I'm that busy.

ALBERT Where do you go now?

HARRY A little fellow on Duncan Street.

ALBERT Duncan Street?

HARRY Ay. Little Indian feller on Duncan Street. Next to the confectioner's.

ALBERT Dear do now, haircut. How much do they charge?

HARRY Sixty p.

ALBERT Sixty p? By –! It's shocking.

HARRY I used to go on East Parade. Mr Batty. I went in there one morning and there's a bloody lass having her hair done. I said, 'What's this?' The lad says, 'We've gone unisex.' I says, 'Unisex? Where's Mr Batty, then?' He says, 'Retired.' I says, 'Retired? He was only about fourteen.' 'Well,' he says, 'he's in Garstang. Furthermore,' he says, 'what with the expense of going unisex, we have been compelled to withdraw our concessions to pensioners.' I came away.

ALBERT They want reporting.

HARRY What do they want with unisex in Morecambe?

ALBERT It's like these sauna baths. They're popping up all over now. Sauna baths. Who's going to patronise sauna baths in Morecambe? Folk aren't coming to Morecambe for sauna baths.

Colin comes up.

COLIN Can you change ten p, please?

ALBERT What do you want it for?

COLIN Five p for the telescope.

ALBERT No. I can't. Here. Here's five p. I'll treat you.

COLIN Ta.

ALBERT (*calling after him*) What're you wanting to see? T'sea?

HARRY You shouldn't have given him that. He'll only look at the lasses on the beach.

ALBERT He's too young for that.

HARRY There's no too young nowadays. They start at ten year old.

ALBERT I wished I'd have started at ten. I were wed at seventeen.

HARRY Ay.

Albert gets up and goes over to Colin and the telescope.

ALBERT Let's have a look. (*He peers through.*) By –! That's marvellous. Oh. T'beggar's clicked off. Short do.

EXT. BEACH. DAY.

Mam and Dad are both asleep.

JENNIFER Mam. Mam. *Mam.*

MAM What?

JENNIFER Take us for a paddle.

MAM It's miles.

JENNIFER Go on, Mam.

The two of them begin to walk towards the sea. It is a long long way over the wet sand.

EXT. SEASHORE. DAY.

MAM Morecambe is where your dad and me did our courting.

JENNIFER I liked Benidorm.

MAM There's no question of Benidorm now.

JENNIFER I liked it.

They have come to the water's edge.

Is this the sea?

MAM I think so.

JENNIFER Where are the cliffs?

MAM There aren't cliffs here.

JENNIFER The book said cliffs.

MAM Not at Morecambe. This is the water's edge.

JENNIFER Is this the proper sea?

MAM Yes.

JENNIFER Paddle with me.

MAM I am paddling with you.

JENNIFER Paddle in the sea.

They do so. Then turn and walk on the sands. Suddenly a sand yacht passes, with a young man on it, brown and beautiful and laughing. It should be wonderful, like something out of a television commercial. It is a vision.

MAM Mustn't that be wonderful?

JENNIFER Can we go on one?

MAM No. We'd better go back. Your dad will be wondering where we've got to.

INT. ICE-CREAM PARLOUR. DAY.
A timid-looking man is waiting. The woman is a long time coming. Colin is waiting behind the man.

MAN What sort is there?

WOMAN There's strawberry, raspberry, vanilla, chocolate peppermint, caramel and blackcurrant.

MAN Is there coffee?

WOMAN (*calling to another waitress*) Gloria. It's going to be one of those days.

EXT. STREET. DAY.
Cut to Colin walking along eating ice cream.

EXT. PIZZA PARLOUR/FISHING-LINE SHOP. DAY.
Colin looks at the money he has left. He hesitates outside the pizza parlour. Then goes into a shop selling fishing lines. He comes out without one. He looks at the fishing lines on display. The shopkeeper comes and stands in the doorway watching him. Colin walks on.

EXT. BOATING POOL. DAY.
A middle-aged man is sailing a motor yacht. He sails it towards him. Colin watches him. Then walks round to meet it. Another boy is also watching.

MAN (*who speaks without looking at him*) Would you like to work it? Are you mechanically minded?

COLIN Yes. No.

MAN Fancy being a sailor? I've got a whole fleet at home. Isn't she beautiful? What's your name?

COLIN Colin.

MAN What's your friend's name?
  Colin looks at the other boy, Graham.
COLIN I don't know. He's not with me.
  Colin sets his course across the pool and the three of them walk round to meet it.
GRAHAM Let's have a go then.
  He winks at Colin behind the man's back and sets the course of the boat straight for a breakwater, which it hits and turns over.
MAN Don't do that. What did you do that for?
GRAHAM What're you laking with boats for, you? You're as old as my dad.
  He walks away with Colin.
  He's a queer. He's always there. He's been had up. (*Shouts.*) Poof!

EXT. BATHING HUTS. DAY.
Colin and Graham are behind a row of bathing huts. Graham is going along, looking in spy-holes in the back of the huts. He beckons to Colin to look.
COLIN She's old.
GRAHAM She's bare. Can you see it?
COLIN No.
GRAHAM Let's see. I can. I saw it.
COLIN Let's see.
GRAHAM She's got her cossie on now.
  They peep at the woman as she comes out in her bathing costume.
GRAHAM It's when two go in you want to be there.
COLIN Yes.
GRAHAM I've seen that. Fantastic. What's your name?
COLIN Colin. What's yours?
GRAHAM Graham.

EXT. JETTY. DAY.
Colin and Graham are walking along the jetty. There are people fishing. They watch them, catching nothing.
GRAHAM It's boring, fishing. Fishing's boring. Fastening it on, taking it off. Waiting. It's boring.
  They walk on.

49

EXT. JETTY. DAY.
GRAHAM What you want a fishing line for?
COLIN I've lost something.
GRAHAM You want to nick one.
COLIN No.
GRAHAM Yes.
COLIN Who off?

EXT. JETTY. DAY.
Cut to a boy crying, running down the jetty. Colin and Graham running away, Colin trailing a line and winding it up as he runs.

EXT. BOARDING HOUSE. DAY.
Cut to Colin approaching the boarding house. Entering the front door very cautiously. There is no one about, but a distant sound of talking from the back room. He goes upstairs.

INT. BOARDING HOUSE: COLIN'S AND JENNIFER'S ROOM. DAY.
Colin opens the window. The shoe is still lying on the flat roof below.

INT. BOARDING HOUSE: CATTLEYS' ROOM. DAY.
Cut to landlady's room. Mr and Mrs Cattley. Long pause.
MR CATTLEY It's not a man's job. Sitting in the launderette.
    They're all women. Apart from me. Washing sheets. I won't go.
MRS CATTLEY If you don't, I'm cutting off your intercommunica-
    tion system. 'The Portofino Room is now open for the service
    of high tea.' What's wrong with a gong? I can remember when I
    used to shout up the stairs.
MR CATTLEY They won't take that now. Shouting up the stairs.
    Gongs. You have to have that Riviera feel.
MRS CATTLEY Listen, we're half-empty. So much for the Riviera
    feel.
MR CATTLEY Everywhere's half-empty this year. It's down all
    over. (*He sees a child's shoe slowly ascending outside the window.*)
    Denise. (*He touches her arm.*)
MRS CATTLEY Don't Denise me. And none of that either. I don't
    want any of that. There's too much of that goes on in this
    place. No wonder we're running to the launderette every five
    minutes.

MR CATTLEY Denise.
She looks.

INT. BOARDING HOUSE: COLIN'S AND JENNIFER'S BEDROOM.
DAY.
COLIN It's our Jennifer's shoe. It fell out of the window.
MRS CATTLEY Fell? Chucked, more like. Why didn't you ask us
  for it? We have access to the roof.
MR CATTLEY Ask us for it, that's right. Access, no problem.
COLIN I didn't think.
MRS CATTLEY Didn't your mother think?
MR CATTLEY Didn't she think? We're not inhuman, are we,
  Denise?
MRS CATTLEY That could go through the double glazing. And do
  you know what that is? Two hundred pounds down the drain.
MR CATTLEY It could go in somebody's eye. And what does the
  insurance say then? 'Fishing for sandals outside the bedroom
  window. Not covered by the policy, Mr Cattley. Not in the
  small print.'

INT. BOARDING HOUSE: CORRIDOR/STAIRS. DAY.
They are coming out of the bedroom and coming downstairs.
MRS CATTLEY Yes, all right, Percy. Where does your mam think
  you are?
COLIN I don't know.
MRS CATTLEY Well, I shall tell her.
MR CATTLEY I shall tell her.
MRS CATTLEY I'll tell her, Percy. Why aren't you out enjoying
  yourself, instead of being stuck inside fishing for sandals? I'm
  keeping this to give to your mother.
COLIN It's our Jennifer's.
MR CATTLEY We shall give it to your mother. Show her what
  you've been up to.
COLIN She's only got that pair. She can't have another pair.
  My dad's . . .
MRS CATTLEY Your dad's what?
COLIN My dad says.
MR CATTLEY Your dad says, why?
MRS CATTLEY What's the matter with your dad?

COLIN Nothing.

MR CATTLEY What about him?

MRS CATTLEY What is it?

COLIN Nothing. He's out of work.

He breaks free and runs off down the stairs and out. The honeymoon couple are coming upstairs – past the Cattleys.

KEITH She's got a headache.

JO I've got a headache.

INT. BOARDING HOUSE: KITCHEN. DAY.

MRS CATTLEY Out of work and coming on holiday. That's not going to get the country back on its feet. Losing shoes.

MR CATTLEY He could just have told me. There would have been no problem. I could have broadcast an appeal.

MRS CATTLEY Out of work. That's the sort of clientele *we* get. That's your 'Riviera feel'.

EXT. BEACH. DAY.

The tide is coming in and the beach has got more crowded. Colin gets back just as the family are beginning to pack up.

MAM Where've you been?

COLIN Nowhere.

DAD Carry this then. Jennifer. Come on.

Jennifer kicks over her sandcastle before going.

EXT. PROMENADE. DAY.

Mr and Mrs Thornton are sitting on the prom. They are chatting to the Coopers.

MR THORNTON No, we haven't done much. We had a little look round Marks and Spencer's, then we sat in a shelter for a bit. We thought we'd take it easy today since we're going to Grange tomorrow.

DAD You do right.

MRS THORNTON It's all so hectic. Even Morecambe. I've watched this place get hectic. It's going to be like the South of France soon.

MR THORNTON There's a hell-hole. 'Course you generally go there.

They get up and walk along the prom with Mam and Dad and Jennifer.

MAM It's been more Spain. But I think you're right, Spain's spoilt now. It's been an eye-opener to me, this holiday. You can have just as good a time at home.

MR THORNTON That's right. Holidays at Home.

DAD Colin. Keep up. Come on.

There is another family walking ahead of them. It is the boy, Derek, whose fishing line Colin has taken. Colin has seen him. Derek looks round. Says something to his father. The Father looks back. Derek looks back again. He stops and they catch up.

DEREK'S FATHER Is this your lad?

DAD Which? Colin? Yes. Why?

DEREK'S FATHER Does he generally thieve, then?

DAD Thieve?

DEREK'S FATHER Thieve. Nick. Lift.

DAD How do you mean, thieve?

MAM Dad, what's the matter?

DEREK'S FATHER He pinched our Derek's fishing line, didn't he, Derek?

DEREK Him and another one. The other one hit me.

MAM Well, we don't have another one.

The Thorntons listen to this exchange.

MRS THORNTON (*mouthing*) We'll go on.

The Thorntons leave.

DEREK'S FATHER He says it was him.

DEREK Yes.

COLIN I didn't.

DEREK'S FATHER He says he did.

DAD Well, he says he didn't.

DEREK'S FATHER Look in his pockets.

DAD Look in your pockets.

COLIN I've looked in my pockets.

DAD Look again.

DEREK'S FATHER Let me look in his pockets.

DAD Don't you touch him.

DEREK'S FATHER Well, I don't know.

One mother smiles uneasily at the other mother, both somewhat embarrassed and not knowing what to do.

He's not that sort of a lad.

DAD Nor is our Colin. You're sure?

COLIN Course I'm sure.

DEREK'S MOTHER Well, come on then. It may not be him.

DEREK It is him.

DEREK'S MOTHER Shut up. Flaming fishing line.

EXT. ROAD TO BOARDING HOUSE. DAY.

They continue back to the digs. Much of this shot on Colin's face.

MAM That kid. Telling t'tale. He was just trying it on. 'Look in his pockets.' I'd have clouted him. Going up to people in the street. Fishing. He was fishing. That's what he was doing. Then showing us up in front of Mr and Mrs Thornton. You'll have to tell them it was all a mistake or it'll be all over the digs.

DAD Never heed. Kids. I don't know.

INT. BOARDING HOUSE: HALL/STAIRS. DAY.

They go into the hall of the boarding house, and begin to go upstairs. Two flights. Slowly. As they get to the bedroom, the tannoy goes.

MR CATTLEY (*over the tannoy*) Would Mr Cooper please come to Reception. Mr Cooper to Reception, please.

Dad turns and goes down again.

INT. BOARDING HOUSE: COLIN'S AND JENNIFER'S BEDROOM. DAY.

Colin is alone in the bedroom.

DAD (*out of vision*) Colin. Colin.

COLIN What?

INT. BOARDING HOUSE: LANDING OUTSIDE COLIN'S AND JENNIFER'S BEDROOM. DAY.

DAD Open me this door. Open me this door.

Mam is at the head of the stairs watching.

COLIN (*out of vision*) I won't.

DAD You will. You bloody well will.

MAM Dad.

Dad gets up on a chair and looks impotently through the glass pane above the door. He gets down and goes away.

INT. BOARDING HOUSE: COLIN'S AND JENNIFER'S BEDROOM. DAY.

A little knock on the door.

JENNIFER (*out of vision*) Colin. Can I come in?

COLIN No.

JENNIFER (*out of vision*) Go on.
DAD (*out of vision, whispering*) Say you want your teddy.
JENNIFER (*out of vision*) I want my teddy.
COLIN Bugger teddy.
JENNIFER (*out of vision*) Go on. Colin. Go on.

INT. BOARDING HOUSE: LANDING OUTSIDE COLIN'S AND
JENNIFER'S BEDROOM. DAY.
*Colin opens it. It is instantly pushed open. Dad springs in and starts
hitting him. Mam waits on the half-landing below, hearing but not
seeing.*
MAM Dad, Dad. Don't hit him on his head, Dad.
DAD Showing us up. I'll give you fishing line. Why didn't you say?
  All you have to do is say. The sandal dropped out of the
  window. Full stop. Can we get it? Full stop. 'Stead of which
  you go pinching fishing lines, and spreading it around I'm
  unemployed. Well, I'm employed now, doing something useful
  for a change.
  Keith comes out, half-dressed, and comes up the stairs.
  Yes?
KEITH Nothing. I just wondered what was going on.
DAD Nothing's going on. Family life's going on. Happily ever
  after's going on. Marriage. Kids. That's what's going on.
KEITH Sorry.
DAD Just got married, have you? Magic, is it? Bliss? Well, take a
  good look, because you'll come to it before you know where
  you are. And don't you be looking so suited, our Jennifer, or
  I'll fetch you one and all. Flaming sandal. You make life more
  complicated. We're trying to make life easy and you're making
  it more complicated. Get in there.
  He flings Colin into the bedroom and shuts the door on him.

INT. BOARDING HOUSE: COLIN'S AND JENNIFER'S BEDROOM. DAY.
Colin lies on the bed, crying.

INT. BOARDING HOUSE: PORTOFINO ROOM. DAY.
*The dining room is empty apart from Fay. And the happy couple –
the older woman, the young man – Hilda and Leslie, sitting by the
window.*

MR CATTLEY (*over the tannoy*) ... for starters, orange juice, grapefruit juice, grapefruit segments or melon balls, followed by duck à l'orange, fresh Norfolk peas and sauté potatoes. For afters we have a second chance to sample Mrs Cattley's famous home-made trifle, plus wafer-thin mints and a choice of beverages.

INT. BOARDING HOUSE: COLIN'S AND JENNIFER'S BEDROOM. DAY.
Colin is sitting by the window, looking out over the roofs and through the chimney pots and television aerials to the distant glitter which is the sea.

One Fine Day

CAST AND CREDITS

One Fine Day was first transmitted by London Weekend Television
on 17 February 1979. The cast included:

WELBY	Robert Stephens
BLAKE	Benjamin Whitrow
STEELE	Edward de Souza
MARSH	Toby Salaman
BLOUNT	Harold Innocent
PHILLIPS	Dave Allen
RYCROFT	Dominic Guard
MISS VENABLES	Joan Scott
AVRIL	Mary Maddox
SANDRA	Liz Crowther
CHRISTINE	Sheila Kelley
FIRST MAN IN LIFT	Hugh Fraser
SECOND MAN IN LIFT	Bill Paterson
THIRD MAN IN LIFT	Gregory Floy
MRS PHILLIPS	Barbara Leigh-Hunt
JENNIFER	Madeleine Church
ROBIN PHILLIPS	Patrick Bailey
COMMISSIONAIRE	Leslie Sands
MISS MORPETH	Rosamund Greenwood
LINDA	Suzanna Hamilton
ARNOLD	Don Fellows
MILTON	Bruce Boa
MR ALPERT	Antony Sher
JUNE	Rebecca Frayn

Produced and directed by	Stephen Frears
Designed by	Frank Nerini
Music by	George Fenton

PART ONE

INT. FROBISHER, RENDELL & ROSS: BOARDROOM. DAY.
The offices of a large London estate agents. A dozen or so men sitting round a long table. It is towards the end of a meeting and the table is strewn with papers. Briefcases by their chairs. Much of the meeting shot from the point of view of Phillips, a man in his late forties. Welby, the Chairman, is turning over various folders.

WELBY What about Fordyce Road? Have we had any feedback there?

BLAKE The odd nibble. No real joy to speak of.

STEELE I think Fordyce Road is maybe a sleeper.

MARSH It's certainly that.
  There is uneasy laughter, which Welby silences with a wide smile.

BLAKE No, seriously, Charles, *au sujet de* Fordyce Road, I think you may find me coming back to you round about Wednesday.

STEELE Hint, hint.

BLAKE The odd feeler, you know.

WELBY Jolly good. Joll–ll–y good. Well, Charles, we'll keep everything crossed on that one, shall we? (*Turns over more folders.*) Compass House. We've done all that. Contracts exchanged when did you say, Rupert?

BLOUNT Tuesday.

WELBY Tuesday, Tuesday, Tuesday. Charles on Tuesday. Maurice on Wednesday. It's all happening, isn't it? Jolly good. Ah. Here's the bluebottle in the Vaseline. Our old friend. Sunley House. (*He has a brochure of the building with a photograph.*) Any glad tidings there, George?
  Phillips shakes his head.
  Glad – ish?

PHILLIPS Not as such.

WELBY Not as such. I see. That's a pity. Because this is the big one.

MARSH It's the big one, all right.

WELBY How long have we had it in the window? A year, is it?

MARSH More like two.

WELBY Two . . . years. One appreciates it's only lately been your pigeon, George, but, you see, what one is . . . a little . . . worried about . . . I say worried, do I mean worried? Yes, I think I do mean worried . . . what one is worried about, George, is that it's getting to look a fraction flyblown. Starting to curl at the edge a bit. Know what I mean?

PHILLIPS Sort of.

Pause.

WELBY Would it help if we could locate the difficulty?

PHILLIPS Lockwood found the same.

WELBY Lockwood was a sick man.

MARSH It's a prime location.

PHILLIPS Oh, sure, it's a prime location.

WELBY Poor Lockwood used to say we would never rent Sunley House until the bottoming-out. Well, we've had the bottoming-out. We had it eighteen months ago. But we're still stuck with Sunley House. Now why, George? I'm genuinely puzzled.

PHILLIPS There is a backlog. Still some highly rentable properties that have been held over. The slack is still in process of being taken up. Our turn will come.

WELBY Turn? Turn, George? You're not suggesting we *wait* our turn?

Pause. He makes this remark a joke – though it isn't a joke – smiling widely at the board meeting, who smile back.

Moreover I was reading in the Pink 'un this morning that there is no slack. The commercial sector is poised. Taut. The crest, as it were, of the wave.

RYCROFT (*an attractive young man of twenty-five*) Yes. I was reading that.

WELBY I once heard Lockwood . . . admittedly it was when he was a very sick man . . . I once heard Lockwood refer to it as 'White Elephant House'. That shocked me, George. Deeply shocked me. And I am wondering if his attitudes haven't, as it were . . . carried over.

PHILLIPS I am sure it will find its own slot, in time.

WELBY In time. In time. I just wish I had your philosophy, George. Your Gaelic philosophy. Time. Hey ho!

RYCROFT Could Residential have a crack at it? If Commercial don't mind, that is.

Phillips deliberately pours water into a glass and shows no sign of answering.

WELBY What say, George?

PHILLIPS It's not been designed for unit occupancy. It was put up in the palmy days when you built first and found a tenant afterwards. Then the money ran out, so the top floor is a shambles.

WELBY Don't show them the top floor.

PHILLIPS I don't. (*Pause.*) Who wants 80,000 square feet of that sort of office space nowadays?

MARSH Our Middle East friends, for a start.

WELBY Quite. All I would say is that I don't think in all honesty there is any point in any of us just sitting on our backsides waiting for the economic climate to do the job for us. The index is on the up and up. Records are being broken, North Sea oil or no North Sea oil, the country is well and truly back on its feet. But we can't sit back. We can't be passengers. It's firms like us that are making that happen. We can't just wait our turn? Time . . . (*slightly mimicking Phillips*) . . . time . . . is of the essence. And that, since it's now after the witching hour of four-thirty, is the message I think we ought to carry away with us. Gentlemen.

Welby chats to Rycroft at the door, obviously waiting to have a word with Phillips, who lingers. The other men come out, nodding and smiling as they come past Welby and the room empties.

RYCROFT Hope I wasn't out of order on that one, sir.

WELBY Absolutely not, Rycroft. Absolutely not. That's what these meetings are for. A monthly powwow. Protocol gets left at the door. Commercial, Residential. Your patch, my patch. Nonsense. The firm, Gerald. Selling. Business. That's what matters. What are toes for but to be trod on? Quite right to speak up.

Welby is seen talking from Phillips's point of view, as Phillips still lingers. To avoid going out he examines a picture on the wall.

PHILLIPS What is that, precisely?

STEELE It's not meant to be anything in particular, is it? One of these abstract jobs.

PHILLIPS Abstract what, though? You like it?

STEELE I'm not frantic about it. Actually I've never really looked at it before. (*He gets interested.*)

PHILLIPS Nor me. I'd say . . . it was probably rubbish.
Welby appears to have gone so Phillips follows Steele out.

INT. FROBISHER, RENDELL & ROSS: CORRIDOR. DAY.
Phillips walks along the corridor behind Blount and Blake.
BLOUNT Lambeth have done another nasty.
BLAKE You surprise me.
BLOUNT Slapped a 416 on Twyford Street.
BLAKE Where's Arthur at this crucial juncture?
BLOUNT Swindon.
BLAKE It never rains. So what's the plan?
BLOUNT No plan. A 416? No *plan*?
BLAKE And where's Arthur?
BLOUNT Swindon.
BLAKE Of course. Well, it's the big decision.
BLOUNT What?
BLAKE Does he put his head in the gas oven there or come back
here and do it?
MISS VENABLES (*she has a tray of flags*) Can I hold you to
ransom? For kidney patients. Dialysis. A wonderful cause.
*Welby has been waiting in a doorway halfway down the corridor,
talking to Marsh. He breaks off instantly to capture Phillips as he
passes. He walks along the corridor with him.*
WELBY My worry is, George, that so long as we've got this place
on our hands it will go on distorting the quarterly estimates.
PHILLIPS I appreciate that.
WELBY I think you do appreciate that. I think you do appreciate
it. But I don't want Central to run away with the impression
we're dragging our feet over this one. At the same time I don't
want to have to spell it out then have Glover ringing up saying,
'Sorry, no understand problem.' You've got acres of room
leasewise. When you think what we're forking out in interest
alone, nobody's going to complain if you come right down.
I'm not suggesting you do come right down, but if it gets it off
our hands . . . (*Awkward silence.*) Anyway . . . How are things
on the family front? Elizabeth well?
PHILLIPS Fine.
WELBY How are the lampshades?

PHILLIPS Conversational Spanish now.
WELBY That's interesting.

INT. FROBISHER, RENDELL & ROSS: OUTER OFFICE/PHILLIPS'S
OFFICE. DAY.
*Three secretaries, Christine, Sandra and Avril, at three desks. Christine
is on the phone.*
AVRIL Well, a daiquiri basically is lime juice, Bacardi rum, sugar
and a dash of maraschino. Only that's really only the bare
essentials. The art is what you put into it besides. When I was
in Corfu with Lynne we had cherry daiquiris.
Sandra's phone rings.
SANDRA I don't dislike Riesling. Have you had that? Frobisher,
Rendell and Ross . . . I rather think Mr Welby is in a meeting at
this moment
At this point, Welby and Phillips come in.
Hang on, I'll just check. (*mouthing at Welby*) Mr Crookshank.
Welby pulls a face and shakes his head.
No, I'm afraid he's in a meeting . . . He'll be tied up now for
the rest of the afternoon. Does he have your number? . . .
Goodbye.
*Christine's conversation on the phone should be heard only in the
background.*
CHRISTINE Brenda said I was a fool and was he index-linked?
Well, I never asked but you can't go building your life on
somebody else's pension prospects, can you? But I think you're
right about beards. I mean they were all right when they were
just starting, but now everybody's got them they've lost their
distinction.
Welby and Phillips appear.
Hold on just one second.
She puts her hand over the phone and waits for Welby to go.
WELBY Rycroft's a bright spark, isn't he? I like him. I like him.
Well. These things are sent to try us. Press on. Press on. (*He
smiles at the typists.*) Don't tell me. Don't tell me. Miss . . .
(*Searches for Avril's name.*) Williamson, no, as you were, as you
were . . . Hopkins . . . ?
Avril turns round the name card on her desk. It is Hopkins.

Where's Miss Williamson now? Reading?

AVRIL Cirencester.

WELBY Cirencester!

He goes away smiling. Christine, Phillips's secretary, is still on the telephone. We see Phillips pass her and take some papers she hands him without stopping talking. The scene is shot on Phillips.

CHRISTINE (*out of vision*) Are you still there? No. He keeps threatening to take me to this topless steak-house. Aylesbury. And he makes out that's a treat for *me*. Besides it's so old-fashioned. People don't go on about topless now. It's really sixties is topless. He's a bit sixties actually. I like him but he is sixties. Stuart. It's a sixties name. A little Fiaty thing. I think. Else it's a Renault. I don't know about cars. Red. Calls it Clarence. Not sure I like that. It's a bit silly, studenty. No. Works for the council. Anyway, Mr Phillips has just come in . . . my lord and master . . . yes . . . just entered. I'd better dash. Yes. No. Don't work too hard.

Phillips signs the papers. Reads and signs. Reads and signs. Gives them to Christine.

PHILLIPS That it?

CHRISTINE Cheer up.

PHILLIPS I'm all right. End of the day.

He gets his coat from the stand and goes out.

INT. FROBISHER, RENDELL & ROSS: CORRIDOR. DAY.
Phillips goes along the corridor. He passes an office where Marsh and Blount are checking through a list.

MARSH 16 Dickinson Road.

BLOUNT 16 Dickinson Road.

MARSH 27 Wadham Gardens.

BLOUNT 27 Wadham Gardens.

MARSH 45 Montague Place.

BLOUNT 45 Montague Place.

MARSH 2 Queen Mary's Road.

Pause.

BLOUNT 2 Queen Mary's Road.

MARSH Hillcrest, Wilton Avenue.

BLOUNT Hillcrest, Wilton Avenue.

MARSH Hewer House. 16 and 17.

BLOUNT 16 and 17 Hewer House.

> *And so on, as long as necessary. At some point during this list,*
> *Blount should see Phillips pass.*

You off?

> *Phillips nods and raises a hand.*

All right for some. (*Then he goes on with the list.*)

INT. FROBISHER, RENDELL & ROSS: LIFT. DAY.

Fairly large and crowded. People staring straight front and watching
the floor indicator. Two men talk in a half-undertone. Much of this shot
on Phillips.

FIRST MAN Bit of an eccentric apparently. Set off to walk right
across Europe in a straight line. The Alps, everything. Ended
up having a paddle in the Mediterranean.

SECOND MAN Yes? Wish I'd seen that.

> *The lift stops at a floor. Conversation ceases and starts again when*
> *the lift starts.*

Some trek.

FIRST MAN I'll say.

ANOTHER VOICE Hit three for me somebody.

FIRST MAN Of course he wouldn't be on his own.

SECOND MAN No?

FIRST MAN You'd have the camera, the producer, the whole bag
of tricks.

THIRD MAN (*getting off*) Gangway! Let the dog see the rabbit.

> *Lift stops. Conversation stops as before.*

SECOND MAN Didn't tempt you, then?

FIRST MAN What?

SECOND MAN To set off on your travels?

FIRST MAN Get out my rucksack.

SECOND MAN Shorts.

FIRST MAN I like to think I'm needed.

SECOND MAN Yes. Break Personnel's heart.

FIRST MAN Heart!

> *Lift stops and everyone gets off, including Phillips. Other faces*
> *expressionless or half-smiles.*

EXT. SUNLEY HOUSE. DAY.
*Phillips outside a tall office block, which is empty and the forecourt
dilapidated. Litter. His car is parked. Some graffiti sprayed on the wall.
He peers in. View into the interior of the building from outside. Dim
vistas, with reflection from outside. View of Phillips from inside the
building, looking at it.*

INT./EXT. PHILLIPS'S CAR/SUBURBAN COUNTRYISH ROAD. DAY.
*Phillips driving home. No other traffic. He brakes hard and stops. Gets
out. Goes back. He has run over a hedgehog. He touches it gingerly
with his foot, grimacing slightly. It isn't dead. Phillips in the car,
reversing. He winces as the car goes over it again. Drives forward
again. Stops, but doesn't get out. Drives on.*

INT. PHILLIPS'S HOME: KITCHEN. EVENING.
*Phillips, with his wife, a slightly scatty woman in her forties, his son,
Robin, and a silent girl, Jennifer. They are having supper.*
MRS PHILLIPS It's the pottest of luck, I'm afraid. I was rushing
  round to get to my class. Does Jennifer want some salad?
  Robin looks at Jennifer. Jennifer slightly shakes her head.
  Apparently Jennifer's father has a market garden.
PHILLIPS A market garden?
JENNIFER It's actually more of a nursery than a market garden.
MRS PHILLIPS I imagine that must be very satisfying. Growing
  things.
ROBIN Is it?
JENNIFER Is it what?
ROBIN Very satisfying?
JENNIFER I don't know.
ROBIN Anybody going to eat this? (*the last potato*)
MRS PHILLIPS Offer it to Jennifer.
ROBIN Jennifer, do you want this?
  She mutely shakes her head.

A little later in the meal.
PHILLIPS I ran over a hedgehog tonight.
  Pause.
MRS PHILLIPS You see so many killed. I suppose it's their own
  fault. Why do they cross the road?

ROBIN Why does the hedgehog cross the road!

JENNIFER They . . .

The table waits.

. . . they have fleas.

ROBIN How would you know?

JENNIFER I do know. They have fleas.

PHILLIPS They do have fleas.

ROBIN Oh, well, if Dad says so.

JENNIFER They're smothered in fleas.

Pause.

I'm doing O Level Biology.

MRS PHILLIPS Shall we stack?

A little later.

MRS PHILLIPS (*to Robin and Jennifer*) Go through. I'll bring
coffee in.

They are stacking the dishwasher.

It's only a week. Ten days at the most. Father's so difficult now,
Betty ought to have a break. (*Pause.*) She *is* my sister.

PHILLIPS I've said. I can manage.

MRS PHILLIPS You are lucky. Having no parents. Dragging on.
You don't know you're born. Anyway if I stock up the freezer.
You can fend. You'll probably rather enjoy it.

PHILLIPS Probably.

MRS PHILLIPS It'll mean missing a couple of my classes.

PHILLIPS That's a pity.

MRS PHILLIPS I'm really revelling in them now. I thought at first
I wasn't going to, as I didn't like the instructor much . . . though
I suppose he's got a point. He just didn't want the course
cluttered up with well-meaning people.

*She starts up the coffee grinder so that what she says next is totally
inaudible to Phillips, just her mouth moving. Once the grinding is
done she becomes audible again.*

. . . though as he says, patience is half the battle, and it's often
a matter of just sitting and sitting there while they puzzle it
out, but there does come a point when the technical training
will come in handy, you know. Well, it's not technical really.
Practical, I suppose I mean. Sympathy's all very well, but
teaching is what they want.

PHILLIPS Sorry. What is this?

MRS PHILLIPS Dyslexics. People who can't read. There's a
woman there, nice-looking woman, comes in a car. Thirty
probably, thirty-five, hard to tell: she cannot read a word.
I said, 'Well, what about the Highway Code?' She said her
husband read it to her and she memorised it. 'Bus Stop' she
can recognise, and 'Exit' – and that's about all. Terrible. You
never think.

PHILLIPS Never think what?

MRS PHILLIPS I don't know. Other people's lives.

PHILLIPS She seems a nice girl.

MRS PHILLIPS Who?

PHILLIPS This girl. Jennifer.

MRS PHILLIPS Yes. Shy. But I like that.

PHILLIPS Why does he want to bring her home?

MRS PHILLIPS It's natural.

PHILLIPS It's not natural. It's not natural at all. I never did.
I don't want to see her.

MRS PHILLIPS I think it's nice he feels able to. Rather touching. I
think maybe . . . she's going to stay the night.

PHILLIPS Where're you putting her? (*Pause.*) Oh, I see.

MRS PHILLIPS I was supposed to ask you.

PHILLIPS Why me?

MRS PHILLIPS If you minded. Do you mind?

PHILLIPS I don't know. Do you?

MRS PHILLIPS Doesn't bother me. I mean these days.

PHILLIPS He's still at school. So is she.

MRS PHILLIPS I was rather touched him asking. It's probably
happened before when we've not been here. I think he just
wants us to approve. (*She has the coffee tray ready.*) You coming
in?

PHILLIPS In a minute.

She goes in, leaving him sitting there.

INT. PHILLIPS'S HOME: LOUNGE. NIGHT.
*A big room. Fairly dark. Pools of light. Stockbroker Tudor. Phillips is
sitting at one end of the room where there is a stereo. The other three are
round the fireplace. Phillips has headphones on, so all we can hear is
the music in his headphones, while seeing some sort of conversation*

going on. He is listening to Madame Butterfly. *There is some looking over towards his end of the room, and eventually Robin walks across and stands in front of him saying something, but we just see his lips moving and can't hear. Phillips takes the headphones off.*

PHILLIPS Sorry?

ROBIN We were just saying goodnight, Dad.

PHILLIPS Oh. Yes. Goodnight. Goodnight.

The second goodnight is to Jennifer, who is waiting unselfconsciously near the door. The boy and girl go, while Mrs Phillips sits smiling placidly on the sofa, and Phillips stares into space, the sound of the opera coming tinnily through the headphones on his lap.

INT. PHILLIPS'S HOME: BEDROOM. NIGHT.

Phillips and Mrs Phillips are getting ready for bed.

PHILLIPS Doesn't she have parents?

MRS PHILLIPS She said. They have this market garden. You should have said if you'd minded.

PHILLIPS I don't mind. You'd think they'd mind: too busy with the yellow sprouting broccoli. You're the one I'd have thought would have minded.

MRS PHILLIPS Why me? I don't mind. I think it's rather nice. I think it's rather a compliment.

PHILLIPS Who to?

MRS PHILLIPS To us. To the way we've brought him up. If it's not here it's somewhere else. The back of the car.

PHILLIPS I'd never have brought anybody home. Not for the night.

MRS PHILLIPS Your childhood was different.

PHILLIPS Why?

MRS PHILLIPS Well – Ireland.

In bed, a little later.

PHILLIPS It's not in bad taste?

MRS PHILLIPS What?

PHILLIPS I just wondered if it was in bad taste.

The house is silent.   •

INT. PHILLIPS'S HOME: BEDROOM. DAWN.

Some noise has awakened Phillips. Maybe it's a cry, but if so it's almost before the scene starts so that it may have been in his sleep or

*elsewhere in the house. His wife is asleep. He lies awake. Listening. He
gets up and looks out into the garden. Dawn. No sound in the house.*

INT. PHILLIPS'S HOME: ROBIN'S BEDROOM. DAWN.
*From Jennifer's point of view, we see Phillips in his dressing gown
standing in the garden. Jennifer, naked, is looking out of the window.
Phillips turns and sees her.*
JENNIFER There's somebody in the garden.
ROBIN (*leaning up on one elbow and looking*) It's only Dad.
JENNIFER He saw me.
ROBIN So what? Stroke my back.

INT. SUNLEY HOUSE: GROUND FLOOR. DAY.
*A group of men, Phillips among them, is walking towards the entrance
door at the end of the ground-floor lobby. They are talking, and we hear
talking but not what they are saying.*
*We are seeing this from the point of view of a Commissionaire in
British Legion uniform. He watches the party go out of the door, at
which he limps over and locks the doors with a lock and chain round
the handles.*
*As the party drives away Phillips comes back and knocks on the glass,
mouthing something we can't hear. The Commissionaire laboriously
unlocks the door again.*
PHILLIPS I don't have my briefcase. I must have left it upstairs.
    (*He walks towards the lift.*)

INT. SUNLEY HOUSE: LIFT. DAY.
Phillips alone in the lift.

INT. SUNLEY HOUSE: UPPER FLOOR. DAY.
*Phillips on the upper floor where he has left his briefcase. We see for the
first time the vista of the empty floor. The rows of telephones. An echo of
the Puccini he was listening to at home. He is obviously taken with the
place.*

INT. SUNLEY HOUSE: TOP FLOOR. DAY.
*Phillips goes through the fire exit and goes upstairs to the unfinished
floor. The floor is uncarpeted and still strewn with builders' debris.
Phillips walks round it. Looks out of the window. There is a view on to*

the rooftop of the next building where there is a little one-storey house,
palings, a pram, potted plants and washing out. A young woman rocks
the pram. A young man waters the plants. Phillips sits down, smiling.

INT. SUNLEY HOUSE: GROUND FLOOR. DAY.
Commissionaire waiting impatiently below. Phillips joins him and they
walk across to the entrance.
COMMISSIONAIRE We'll go out the bottom way. That's all
    locked, bolted and barred.

INT. SUNLEY HOUSE: STAIRCASE/CORRIDOR/COMMISSIONAIRE'S
OFFICE. DAY.
They are going down a blank, featureless staircase.
COMMISSIONAIRE No nearer.
PHILLIPS Doesn't look like it.
COMMISSIONAIRE They'll not rent it till they get that top floor
    finished. It's just like the builders left it. Builders! All Micks,
    what do you expect? Do with a bit of life though. People
    coming in on a morning. Secretaries. Cleaners. Phones going. I
    used to be over the old Prudential building. My missis goes out
    cleaning. Out at five every morning, back at ten. Done a day's
    work before most folks have even started. Still, our eldest girl's
    a manicurist and we've got a son in West Germany, so we
    haven't done too badly. That's the place by all accounts. Shops
    open whenever you want them. He'll shop at eleven at night
    sometimes. They have a different philosophy there.
PHILLIPS (*waiting by the door of the Commissionaire's room*) You
    don't live on the premises?
COMMISSIONAIRE No fear. Hanwell. That's where I live. Why?
PHILLIPS Nothing.
COMMISSIONAIRE This is my little office. Or will be when you
    lot pull your fingers out.
PHILLIPS Cosy.
    The Commissionaire's office should have an armchair, table, kettle,
    cup. A few bare essentials.
    We'll have the keys to this door, I suppose?
COMMISSIONAIRE Somebody's got one. Security's got one,
    I know that. Coming round with that flaming dog, and many a
    time leaving a right parcel. I shouldn't have to have that to see

to. But that's this country all over. You come through Dunkirk and end up cleaning up after a bloody Alsatian. Trade unions, no thank you.

He closes the door, leaving Phillips standing outside the building.

INT. FROBISHER, RENDELL & ROSS: OUTER OFFICE/PHILLIPS'S OFFICE. DAY.

AVRIL A negroni's nice. Gin, sweet vermouth and Campari. If anybody ever offers you one of them, say yes. I had one in Ipswich once, at the Hole in the Wall.

Christine is inexorably typing and does not stop throughout the scene. Rycroft is sitting on her desk, using the telephone.

RYCROFT What am I doing? You know me, Roger, what do you think I'm doing? I'm stretched out across the desk while Christine drops grapes into my mouth, that's what I'm doing ... Just a routine Tuesday afternoon. What gives in Conveyancing? Yeah? I don't believe that for a start. Anyway, Christine's having problems with my zip so I'll tear myself reluctantly away. Yes. Don't work too hard. (*Puts the phone down.*) Who's he got seeing it today, then?

CHRISTINE Same people who saw it last week.

RYCROFT So they are interested?

CHRISTINE I shouldn't think so for a minute. Difficult to adapt to their management structure is what they said. Do you know what that means? Not enough toilets. You're sitting on our *Property Gazette.*

Rycroft takes it out from under him and flicks through it.

RYCROFT Still, they took a second look.

CHRISTINE What's that to you, Mr Nosey Parker? You're Residential Properties. This is Commercial. Just mind your own business.

RYCROFT Come on, Christine.

CHRISTINE Don't come on Christine me. My name isn't June Glazier. Besides which there's a computer programmer in Aylesbury worships the ground I walk on, so get your bum off my desk and get back where you belong. Sod it, you've made me go on treble spacing.

AVRIL Then there's a sidecar, that's lemon juice, brandy and Cointreau. An old-fashioned: whisky, angostura and a lump of sugar. A white lady, that's white of egg, grenadine and gin. Black velvet, that's two parts of Guinness to two parts of champagne . . . I mean it's a whole world. It's my hobby really, cocktails. If I was on *Miss World*, that's what I should have to say . . .

SANDRA What exactly is angostura?

RYCROFT Bahrain. That's the place to be. The Persian Gulf. No fiddling about showing dismal little couples over desirable properties in Cricklewood and Tottenham, and then having to hang about while they do the ritual dance round the building societies to conjure up a mortgage. Abu Dhabi, Kuwait. That's the place to be. They don't know what a mortgage means. They fetch it in bags. Money. Not to mention s–e–x.

Enter Phillips and Rycroft rises unhurriedly.

PHILLIPS Where?

RYCROFT Where what?

PHILLIPS The s–e–x.

RYCROFT Not here.

CHRISTINE Not for want of trying.

RYCROFT I just popped by to say I'd got shot of Lillie Road.

PHILLIPS Who to?

CHRISTINE (*but still typing*) To whom.

RYCROFT Clients. I just pushed the OPP. [*outline planning permission*]

PHILLIPS There's no planning permission on Lillie Road.

RYCROFT It's up to them to find that out.

PHILLIPS OPP. on Lillie Road! They'll be back.

RYCROFT It's the old *caveat emptor.*

PHILLIPS I'll give you ten p if they ever exchange contracts.

RYCROFT What happened at White Elephant House?

PHILLIPS Not keen, the clients. Not over-struck. Seemingly they would have to restructure.

RYCROFT Pity.

PHILLIPS Yes.

RYCROFT I bet I could sell it.

PHILLIPS I imagine you could. But would it stay sold?

INT. FROBISHER, RENDELL & ROSS: CORRIDOR. DAY.
Phillips going along, passing Steele's office. Steele and his secretary, Miss Venables, are going through a list.

MISS VENABLES Ridgeway Mansions, 14 and 26.
STEELE Ridgeway Mansions, 14 and 26.
MISS VENABLES The Parade, Cheshunt.
STEELE The Parade, Cheshunt.
MISS VENABLES Harrogate, Hanaper House.
STEELE Harrogate, Hanaper House.
MISS VENABLES Ilkley, Moorlands Drive.
STEELE Ilkley, Moorlands Drive.
  Pause.
MISS VENABLES Leeds, Harehills.
STEELE Leeds, Harehills.
MISS VENABLES Newark, Foregate Street.
STEELE Newark, Foregate Street.
MISS VENABLES Bodmin, Talgarth Road.
STEELE Bodmin, Bodmin, Bodmin. Bodmin, Talgarth Road.

INT. FROBISHER, RENDELL & ROSS: MISS MORPETH'S OFFICE.
DAY.
Phillips is waiting by the desk of an oldish lady, Miss Morpeth.
MISS MORPETH It's here somewhere.
  She keeps pulling out keys with tattered labels.
  Hardwick Street. No. Prestbury Road.
PHILLIPS Prestbury Road's been sold a long time.
MISS MORPETH Has it? Oh well. You never know when a spare
  key comes in handy. Leamington Street. No. How's Mrs
  Phillips? Cambridge Road. No. How's her bookbinding?
PHILLIPS Flourishing. Flourishing.
  *Miss Morpeth opens her hand and gives him the key with a secret
  smile. He takes it, also smiling as he goes.*
MISS MORPETH (*calling after him*) Mr Phillips. The book. (*Holds
  up an exercise book.*) Have to sign the book.
  *Phillips makes a gesture to indicate he has forgotten, but it is
  exaggerated, though to a very small degree, but enough to show
  that it is false. He had not forgotten. He comes back and signs. Miss
  Morpeth smiles.*
  My system.

INT. FROBISHER, RENDELL & ROSS: GENTS' LOO. DAY.
Blake is having a pee. Blount is inside a cubicle.

BLAKE Why don't we try fifty-seven?

BLOUNT (*out of vision*) Well, it's an interesting figure.

BLAKE A very interesting figure. George.

Phillips has come into the loo.

BLOUNT (*out of vision*) We might even think about fifty-eight.

BLAKE Fifty-eight is less interesting. How's George?

PHILLIPS Flourishing. Flourishing.

BLOUNT (*out of vision*) Is that George? Hello, George.

PHILLIPS Hello, Rupert.

BLAKE Though there is an Aga. And a walled garden.

PHILLIPS Where?

BLOUNT (*out of vision*) Well, there's a garden and there's a wall.
I'm not sure there's a walled garden.

BLAKE Cranleigh.

Blount comes out of the cubicle.

Well, let's try fifty-seven then. Sevenoaks will probably have a
heart attack, but we'll cross that bridge when we come to it.
Age before beauty.

He lets Phillips go out first.

INT. FROBISHER, RENDELL & ROSS: CORRIDOR/LIFT. DAY.

*Phillips comes out of the loo followed by Blake and Blount. He finds
Welby waiting at the lift. Welby immediately collars him.*

WELBY Ah, George. I'm glad I've run across *you*. (*Presses button
for lift.*) I had young Rycroft in earlier on.

Phillips doesn't help him.

The thing is, sometimes I wonder if we're getting a little staid.
I wonder sometimes if a little cross-fertilisation mightn't be
beneficial . . . I told him.

PHILLIPS Who?

WELBY Rycroft.

PHILLIPS Ah, Rycroft.

WELBY I told him he could have a crack at our little problem
child.

PHILLIPS Why?

*The doors open and the lift arrives. They get in. Doors close.
Everybody facing front, looking at floor indicator.*

WELBY (*in slightly conspiratorial tone because overheard*) Why?

PHILLIPS Yes.

WELBY Seemed keen. Is keen. No harm in it. Not poaching.

PHILLIPS Oh no.

Lift stops.

VOICE Ten anybody?

ANOTHER VOICE I'm ten.

VOICE You could have fooled me.

WELBY How's your good lady? How's the carpentry? She put up any more shelves?

PHILLIPS No. I think we're fairly well catered for in the shelf department.

WELBY She's a remarkable woman.

PHILLIPS Yes. She's in Colchester for a few days. Looking after her father.

WELBY Colchester. Really. I once had a Chinese meal there. Well, this looks very much like the ground floor. After you.

INT. SUNLEY HOUSE: TOP FLOOR. SUNSET.
Phillips is sitting on a box in the empty room looking at it. The couple are outside their house. They stand by the pram and kiss. Phillips smiles.

INT. PHILLIPS'S HOME: LOUNGE. EVENING.
Robin and Jennifer are watching television, his arm outstretched behind her on the sofa. Phillips appears through the kitchen door. Robin raises a lazy hand. Sound of television.

INT. PHILLIPS'S HOME: KITCHEN. EVENING.
One place laid. Jennifer comes through.

JENNIFER We had ours.

She starts to get his meal out of the oven.

PHILLIPS I can manage.

She sits down and watches him eat without saying anything, so that he has to keep looking up, giving her uneasy smiles. Robin comes through and stands in the doorway, beside her, his hand on her shoulder.

ROBIN You were late, so we had ours. You remember Jennifer.

PHILLIPS Yes. (*Smiles.*) How was school?

ROBIN I'm not sure. (*Asks Jennifer.*) How was school?

JENNIFER All right. Wasn't it?

ROBIN Yes. All right.

PHILLIPS And what about the yellow sprouting broccoli?

> *She smiles uncomprehendingly. Robin is suspicious he is being got at.*
> In the market garden?

JENNIFER It's more of a nursery really.

Later.
Phillips alone.

INT. PHILLIPS'S HOME: LOUNGE. NIGHT.
Phillips goes through into lounge. Robin and Jennifer are back on the sofa. He sits apart. Watching them without them noticing.

INT. PHILLIPS'S HOME: CORRIDOR. NIGHT.
Phillips gets a canvas holdall.

INT. PHILLIPS'S HOME: ROBIN'S BEDROOM. NIGHT.
Phillips gets a bedroll from Robin's room. He looks at the room. Teddy bear, tin soldiers, stereo, pop posters, all periods of Robin's life represented in the objects there.

INT. PHILLIPS'S HOME: HALL. NIGHT.
Phillips holds the bag now containing the sleeping bag, and waits to see if he should go and say goodnight. Decides against it. Opens the outer door quietly and goes out.

INT. SUNLEY HOUSE: TOP FLOOR. NIGHT.
Phillips is on the unfinished floor he looked at earlier. He is lying on the bed with his eyes open, listening to music on his cassette tape recorder.

PART TWO

INT. SUNLEY HOUSE: TOP FLOOR. EARLY MORNING.
Phillips puts a screen round his bedroll, etc., and leaves the building.

EXT./INT. KEY SHOP. DAY.
The shop advertises 'Keys Cut While-U-Wait'.
PHILLIPS One o'clock? It says while you wait.
WOMAN Well, you can wait, but you don't want to be sat there all
morning, do you?
PHILLIPS What takes so long?
WOMAN He's got arthritis.
PHILLIPS Maybe you ought to alter the sign.
WOMAN We're ready for retiring. We've got to come out of here
anyway. All this is coming down. Is it important? The key.
PHILLIPS It's not important.

INT. FROBISHER, RENDELL & ROSS: MISS MORPETH'S OFFICE. DAY.
MISS MORPETH Well, I can't find it. Mr Phillips did have it but
he signed it back in first thing this morning.
RYCROFT It can't have been lost in that short time. Are you sure
he gave you it?
MISS MORPETH He signed it in the key book. It was before I
came in. (*Shows him book.*) Look. Ticked off returned.
RYCROFT It's pathetic. A firm this size and we have a dirty little
exercise book.
MISS MORPETH We've always had an exercise book.
RYCROFT They're coming from Croydon.
*As Rycroft is talking to Miss Morpeth, Welby appears, coming into
work, a wide smile as ever on his face.*

INT. FROBISHER, RENDELL & ROSS: OUTER OFFICE/PHILLIPS'S
OFFICE. DAY.
Phillips is shaving with an electric razor. Welby puts his head in.
WELBY Ah, George. When you've completed your *toilette*, a word?
*In the background, Avril is typing. Sandra is on the telephone
reading out details of a property.*

SANDRA Four bedrooms, two bathrooms, dining room, family
sitting room, self-contained staff or granny flat. Double garage
and two acres of paddock. And it's sixty-four.

INT. FROBISHER, RENDELL & ROSS: MISS MORPETH'S OFFICE. DAY.
*In the background we can see Miss Morpeth still unhappily searching
for the key. Welby, Phillips and Rycroft talk in a slight undertone in the
foreground.*
WELBY I think Rycroft has a point, that as a system it is lacking
in efficiency or not so much efficiency, I think, as elegance.
The key isn't important in itself, you say the caretaker has one
and Security and after all nobody's going to make off with the
building, more's the pity . . . and you did sign it in?
Phillips nods.
I'm sure, yes . . . so it must be somewhere about. What is
unfortunate is Rycroft has people coming from . . . Coventry?
RYCROFT Croydon.
WELBY Croydon. Not so far.
PHILLIPS Croydon's not the end of the world. They can come
another time.
WELBY They can come another time. Still one doesn't like to get
off on the wrong foot, particularly when Rycroft's been so
quick off the mark. Still. You're sure you returned the . . . of
course you are. Still. The other point is Miss Morpeth, who is
quite plainly not getting any younger, and I wonder whether
she might not be happier doing something a little less
demanding. What do you think?
Phillips's face is blank. Rycroft obviously agrees.
Peggy, perhaps you'd like to pop in and see me this afternoon . . .
*Another secretary looks up, stops typing for a fraction, and then goes
on.*
. . . if that's convenient and we'll try and sort this one out.
(*going*) What with one thing and another this property is
turning out to be a real bugger.

INT. FROBISHER, RENDELL & ROSS: CORRIDOR. DAY.
Miss Venables is coming down the corridor with a small watering can.
MISS VENABLES Morning, Mr Phillips. Morning. How's the
vine? Grapes yet? Mrs Phillips planted a vine.

PHILLIPS Dead.

MISS VENABLES Oh, what a shame. But be sure. Sometimes they look dead, then suddenly they're clambering all over the place. Now can I twist your arm? (*She has a tray of flags.*) Kidney machines. Half an hour each day and they lead a perfectly normal life. They're a real boon.

Phillips forks out. Rycroft is going.

Mr Rycroft, don't escape.

Rycroft has gone.

Fled! Oh, he's young. They don't realise, do they?

FROBISHER, RENDELL & ROSS: OUTER OFFICE/PHILLIPS'S OFFICE. DAY.

Phillips goes back into his office and continues shaving. Rycroft follows him. Christine is already at her typewriter.

PHILLIPS Who are these Croydon people anyway?

RYCROFT Contacts.

PHILLIPS Sorry about that.

RYCROFT Plenty more fish in the sea. Do you generally shave at the office?

PHILLIPS Sometimes.

CHRISTINE First time I've seen it.

PHILLIPS (*looking out of the window*) How funny.

RYCROFT What?

PHILLIPS I was thinking that was a donkey. It's a chair with a coat over it.

RYCROFT Where?

PHILLIPS You can't see it now.

INT. FROBISHER, RENDELL & ROSS: LIFT. DAY.

STEELE Reckon it's an apple and a piece of cheese today.

BLAKE Missing the exercise?

STEELE You know we lost the twelve-thirty slot?

BLAKE So I heard. Good old Graham.

STEELE They were trying to sell us six o'clock.

BLAKE Ha ha.

STEELE I said to Graham, 'Six o'clock's no good to me. Six o'clock and I'm hopefully crawling through Totteridge.'

BLAKE Quite.

STEELE He tends to put people's backs up.
BLAKE He puts *my* back up. I *loved* twelve-thirty.
    Lift stops. Marsh gets in.
MARSH Is four an improvement?
STEELE It's an improvement, Graham, but it's not ideal.
MARSH I know it's not ideal.
BLAKE Twelve-thirty was ideal.
STEELE Ideal.
MARSH Listen, Geoff. Forget twelve-thirty. It was pure fluke we
    ever had twelve-thirty. The twelve-thirty days are over. Twelve-
    thirty! Everybody wants twelve-thirty.
STEELE Graham . . .
MARSH Squash. I don't know why I ever took it on. Twelve-
    thirty.
STEELE Graham . . .
    The lift stops. Marsh gets out.
BLAKE Not a happy man.
STEELE You lunching, George?
PHILLIPS I won't this time, Geoff.
STEELE Hey ho.

EXT. KEY SHOP. DAY.
*Lunch hour. Busy city street. Phillips comes out of the key shop. Looks
at watch.*

INT. FROBISHER, RENDELL & ROSS: OUTER OFFICE/PHILLIPS'S
OFFICE. DAY.
Christine is typing. Phillips comes in.
CHRISTINE Miss Morpeth's in tears in the toilet. Says she's going
    to be sacked.
PHILLIPS She's not going to be sacked.
CHRISTINE She says she is. She thinks it's just a preliminary to
    being computerised.
PHILLIPS How can you computerise keys?
CHRISTINE She says they can computerise anything these days.
    She says if they can computerise Sandra Maynard they can
    computerise her.
PHILLIPS Sandra was estimates. That's different.
CHRISTINE Just what I said through the door. And besides they

didn't computerise Sandra. She just got pregnant about the time they were computerising. It was sheer coincidence. The two weren't connected at all.

PHILLIPS Anyway, they've found the key.

CHRISTINE Oh, yes? Where was it? In your pocket?

PHILLIPS Under her desk. I've spoken to Mr Welby. It's all all right. You'd better go get her out.

CHRISTINE All in good time. I'm stretched across five columns at the moment with a very temperamental tabulator. Do you know who I blame?

Phillips looks out of the window.

PHILLIPS Who?

CHRISTINE Love's Young Dream. Bahrain. He's the one who wants computerising. He was in a minute or two since. Said his people had gone off the boil and whose fault was that. They're now looking at something in Acton.

PHILLIPS (*looking out of the window*) It's very strange. You never think of the city as being built on land. The land underneath the city. Hills, slopes, streams. Trees. These must have been water meadows once. Cattle coming down. Reeds. And not property. *Land.*

CHRISTINE I'll go and rescue Miss Morpeth.

INT. FROBISHER, RENDELL & ROSS: LADIES' LOO. DAY.
Avril and Linda are making up, etc., in front of the mirror. One of the cubicle doors is closed.

AVRIL I am fed up.

LINDA Why?

AVRIL Had this big argument last night with Keith.

LINDA What about?

AVRIL Well, it started as an argument about daiquiris, then it sort of spread to the whole relationship. You see Keith was saying that a daiquiri is a short. And I said it's not a short, it's a cocktail. Cocktails aren't necessarily shorts. I mean a daiquiri's a long drink.

LINDA What did Keith say?

AVRIL Started on about my mother.

Christine comes in. Knocks on the door of the cubicle.

CHRISTINE Peggy. Peggy.

MISS MORPETH (*out of vision*) What?

CHRISTINE It's been found. It's all right.

Miss Morpeth comes out slowly. Avril and Linda puzzled, watching.

INT. SUNLEY HOUSE: TOP FLOOR. DUSK.

Phillips has brewed some coffee. He is carrying the cup and walking round the building. He sees the couple opposite. They are sitting outside enjoying the evening. They kiss.

INT. PHILLIPS'S HOME: CORRIDOR/BEDROOM. NIGHT.

Robin walks along the corridor dressed only in a shirt. He goes into his parents' bedroom. Jennifer is already in bed. He shuts the door.

ROBIN I don't think it's fair.

JENNIFER It's only so's we can sleep. Yours, it's like a doll's bed.

Robin takes off his shirt and gets into bed.

ROBIN It's not fair on Mum.

JENNIFER I dropped off in Maths this afternoon.

ROBIN And what if he comes back?

JENNIFER He's got a girl. Someone else.

ROBIN Dad? Lay off. It's just not fair. I'm surprised you can't see that.

JENNIFER Why?

ROBIN I don't know why.

JENNIFER Don't you like me?

ROBIN What's that got to do with it? It's not fair on me. He should be here. Then everything would be all right. It would be good then.

JENNIFER I like it. The place to ourselves.

ROBIN Anyway, you should be this side.

JENNIFER Why?

ROBIN That's his side.

They slide across one another and change places. Robin is still not happy.

This is wrong too.

They change again. Jennifer puts her hand on his back.

I don't want to do anything. Let's just sleep.

Pause.

He'll probably be here at the weekend. And after that Mum's back.

Jennifer snuggles up to him.
Lay off.

INT./EXT. SUNLEY HOUSE. DAY.
*Various shots of it. Streets around it empty and silent. Top floor. Empty.
The door to the roof open. Sound of church bells.*

EXT. SUNLEY HOUSE: ROOF. DAY.
*A deckchair on the roof, with Phillips sitting there in the sun. A book.
He is half-asleep. His cassette recorder playing.*

EXT. SUNLEY HOUSE. DAY.
A Securicor van draws up.

INT. SUNLEY HOUSE: GROUND FLOOR. DAY.
*Securicor Man with Alsatian dog walking across the entrance hall. His
van visible through the window.*

EXT. SUNLEY HOUSE: ROOF. DAY.
Phillips asleep.

INT. SUNLEY HOUSE: UPPER FLOOR. DAY.
*The Securicor Man coming through the empty floor. Past the lines of
phones. The Alsatian sniffing the phones. The Securicor Man goes up
the stone fire staircase.*

EXT. SUNLEY HOUSE: ROOF. DAY.
Phillips asleep on the roof. Music.

INT. SUNLEY HOUSE: STAIRCASE. DAY.
*The Securicor Man listens. He cannot quite hear the music. The dog
seems to hear something. The dog barks. The Securicor Man goes up the
stairs. The ladder to the roof.*

EXT. SUNLEY HOUSE: ROOF. DAY.
*The roof is empty. The deckchair gone. The Securicor Man locks the
door. Phillips emerges from the central-heating stack carrying his
deckchair. Cautiously he looks over as far below the van drives away.
Then tries door. Locked. He waits. He scouts round the roof. He finds
a cradle with ropes. He starts to take the rope off. He ties the rope round*

a stack to secure it. Then looks over the side. Then sits down. He is terrified.

A little later. Phillips is still sitting there. He gets up, throws the rope with a brick on it to break the first window below the sill. The height makes him dizzy. He sits down again unable to face it. Eventually he lets himself down over the side. He clambers in at the broken window, very very frightened. Once inside some serenity returns. Which turns to pride and pleasure, as he looks down and looks up and sees what he has done.

INT. SUNLEY HOUSE: TOP FLOOR. NIGHT.
Phillips, very happy, goes to sleep.

INT. FROBISHER, RENDELL & ROSS: OUTER OFFICE/PHILLIPS'S OFFICE. DAY.
Next morning. Christine is working at her desk. Phillips comes briskly through the outer office.
PHILLIPS Good morning, good morning, good morning. Morning, girls.
CHRISTINE Good morning. Who shook your cage?
PHILLIPS It's Monday morning, Christine. A new day. A new week. The world, Christine, is our oyster.
CHRISTINE Mrs Phillips not back, is she?
PHILLIPS No, Christine. Wednesday. Meanwhile we have some work to catch up with. The little matter of Sunley House. Number one on the agenda: get on to those Japs and fix up a time for tomorrow. Clear it with Mr Welby, but make it early. Nine.
CHRISTINE Nine. Mr Welby won't like that.
PHILLIPS Good. Number two: check with Costing to see whether they've done a breakdown on the redecorating estimates. Three: get on to Inman and Drury. Tell them I want the plumbing and circuit plans and I want somebody there tomorrow morning who could do snap estimates for possible alterations. Four: take the pillow out of the gas oven. I shan't be needing it. And five . . .
CHRISTINE Yes?
PHILLIPS Not a word to our friend.
CHRISTINE I haven't seen him this morning.

INT. SUNLEY HOUSE. DAY.

Rycroft is showing round three clients. He walks ahead talking to
Arnold. Milton and a tall, silent American bring up the rear.

RYCROFT We are, of course, fully air-conditioned with the latest
in underfloor central heating. The beauty of the building is that
while enjoying this splendid view . . .

ARNOLD Kind of semi-rural, Milton.

MILTON Grass, Arnold.

RYCROFT . . . we are nevertheless only a few minutes from the
centre of town.

ARNOLD That's handy. That's handy, Milton.

MILTON It is handy.

ARNOLD You appreciate, Mr Rycroft, that our problem is . . .
you're kind of young, aren't you, Mr Rycroft? I was just saying
to Mr Rycroft, he's kind of young, Milton.

MILTON He is young, Arnold.

RYCROFT We–ell

ARNOLD No, don't apologise. We like to see that . . . no, our
problem is we have a management structure which is basically
horizontal in layout. And deliberately so in order to maximise
interpersonal contact. Which rightly . . . or possibly wrongly . . .
though I happen to believe rightly . . . is very valuable in
developing a company ethic. Now this property has been
custom-built to house what is basically a vertical management
structure. Having said that, we are at this moment in time
recruiting new personnel so we are still fairly fluid in that area.
But as I say that's something maybe we should want to take
another look at. You don't look more than twenty-four.

RYCROFT That's right. Of course you appreciate we do have
other clients who are very interested. A location of this sort
doesn't turn up every day.

ARNOLD *Naturellement.* When did it become available?

RYCROFT Six months ago. Less.

ARNOLD Funny, I had the idea it was more.

MILTON I had the idea it was more.

ARNOLD Still, I'm very impressed.

MILTON I'm very impressed too.

INT. FROBISHER, RENDELL & ROSS: OUTER OFFICE/PHILLIPS'S OFFICE. DAY.

Christine is on the phone.

CHRISTINE Well, that's what Mr Phillips wants. (*Puts her hand over the phone.*) I'm not getting anywhere. Pick up two.

Phillips picks up the phone.

PHILLIPS Phillips speaking. What's the problem? Yes, well, you don't seem to be getting the message. I want a complete rundown on renovation and possible conversion costs. The details can wait but I want an outline estimate on my desk by five o'clock this afternoon. If you can't do that the contract goes to someone who can, right? I've got clients coming first thing tomorrow morning. I want to be able to quote actual facts and figures and put an estimate in their hands. Right. Right. Now you're beginning to make sense. Oh, and while we're on the subject, I notice we have a broken window. You'd better get on to that.

Christine is lost in admiration.

INT. SUNLEY HOUSE: TOP FLOOR. DAY.

They are looking at the broken window.

RYCROFT All renovations would of course be taken up in the terms of the lease. It must have happened over the weekend.

MILTON We're not in a violent neighbourhood here, Mr Rycroft?

RYCROFT Not a bit.

They go towards the staircase.

ARNOLD Curious place for a window to be broken. Hardly kids.

RYCROFT No.

MILTON A large bird perhaps.

ARNOLD What about the next floor?

RYCROFT I'm not sure . . . if you really need to see it, though of course if you want to . . .

ARNOLD I think we do.

INT. SUNLEY HOUSE: STAIRCASE/TOP FLOOR. DAY.

ARNOLD I gather this top floor is unfurbished. (*calling back down the stairs*) Milton, you appreciate this next floor is unfurbished?

MILTON I've made a note of that, Arnold.

RYCROFT We felt that were it to serve as an executive suite, clients would prefer a free hand with decoration and so on.

ARNOLD (*coming out on to the derelict floor*) Absolutely. I wonder whether . . .

He begins to talk in a more hushed tone to his companions, smiles apologetically at Rycroft, indicating they have to have some discussion among themselves, so Rycroft wanders off. He wanders round the room, eventually ending up at the screen behind which is Phillips's bedroll, etc. The other three are still talking. Rycroft looks out of the window, walks along by the window and finds himself behind the screen. He takes it all in. The bed. The Bible. The cassette. Cut to the other group.

What do you think, Milton?

MILTON What do you think, Arnold?

The third man, who hasn't spoken, is stony-faced.

ARNOLD What do you think, Mr Alpert?

Mr Alpert should suddenly be revealed as the money, Arnold and Milton as minions.

MR ALPERT It's shit.

ARNOLD Mr Rycroft.

Rycroft is behind the screen still. Cut to him still looking at the layout. He has found the yellow flag that Phillips bought from Miss Venables in the office.

RYCROFT Coming.

He takes the flag, and goes over to them as they begin to walk out.

ARNOLD Mr Alpert was just saying you've got a fine property here all in all, a really fine piece of real estate and in its layout and overall format somewhat reminiscent of our Brussels office . . .

INT. FROBISHER, RENDELL & ROSS: LIFT. DAY.
Phillips leaving the building.

PHILLIPS (*brightly*) Another day!

BLOUNT For some of us. Guess where I'm headed. Harlesden. A launderette with great potential for a client with imagination.

BLAKE Sir's just landed me with Hartlepool.

PHILLIPS No problem there. You just plug the environment aspect. Exclusive use of local materials, all trees to remain on site . . .

BLAKE There are no trees. There is no environment.

PHILLIPS Well, invent one. Get the drawing office to run you up an artist's impression. Lots of elegant people sitting about the piazza in the Mediterranean-type sunshine. Better still, give it to Rycroft.

BLOUNT I haven't seen him all day.

BLAKE I suppose it's too much to hope he's died.

PHILLIPS No. Probably just teething. 'Night, all.

INT. SUNLEY HOUSE: TOP FLOOR. DAY.
Rycroft waiting in Phillips's hideout.

EXT. STREETS. DAY.
Phillips walking through the rush-hour streets.

INT. SUNLEY HOUSE: TOP FLOOR. DAY.
Rycroft waiting.

EXT. STREETS NEAR SUNLEY HOUSE. DAY.
Phillips approaching the building.

INT./EXT. SUNLEY HOUSE: LOBBY. DAY.
Phillips comes into the building by his usual entrance, passing the Commissionaire's door, when the Commissionaire suddenly comes out.

COMMISSIONAIRE Now then. Oh. Sorry. Mr Phillips.

PHILLIPS I was just coming in to check. I've got some clients coming tomorrow. You're here late.

COMMISSIONAIRE I'm on watch. We're both of us on watch. Your Mr Rycroft. He's upstairs. Been there all day.

PHILLIPS What for?

COMMISSIONAIRE We've got a squatter. Somebody's done a squat. Here. Camp bed. Sleeping bag. One of these cassette things. The whole bag of tricks. Disgusting.

PHILLIPS Who? How did they get in?

COMMISSIONAIRE It's a mystery. The young fellow was trying to figure it out. Tried to put the blame on me for a start, cocky little sod. It's not my fault. He wants to surprise him. Catch him in the act. Going to stay all night if he has to.

PHILLIPS I'd better leave him to it. Does he know who it is?

COMMISSIONAIRE Don't know. It'll be some nasty little ginger Jesus. Smoking heroin and picking his toenails. It's not as if it's residential accommodation. You don't squat here. You don't squat anywhere. But you don't squat here. Anyway (*leading the way out*) I'm off. I'm not paid for night security. Leave him to it.

He locks the door. Phillips looks at the building.

EXT. PARKLAND. DAY.
We see Phillips sitting on the hill near Alexandra Palace looking at the building. Fairly depressed.

INT. FROBISHER, RENDELL & ROSS: LIFT/OUTER OFFICE/ PHILLIPS'S OFFICE. EVENING.
Phillips goes back to his own office. Up in the empty lift. Through the empty office. Covers on typewriters. Sits at his desk. Very depressed. Thoughtful. Staring out of the window. We see him begin to tidy his desk. Empty the drawers. Pack up. Plainly he thinks Rycroft has found him out and he is finished.

INT. SUNLEY HOUSE: TOP FLOOR. NIGHT.
Rycroft staring out of the window of Sunley House. He sees the couple opposite. They are quarrelling. The young husband hits his wife.

INT. FROBISHER, RENDELL & ROSS: OUTER OFFICE/PHILLIPS'S OFFICE. DAWN.
Desk cleared. Phillips stares out of the window as dawn breaks.

INT. SUNLEY HOUSE. DAY.
The sun shines on the building. Already it looks better. The party is going round. Phillips, Welby and several smiling Japanese. Welby and Phillips are slightly ahead, Phillips very silent.

WELBY Cheer up, George. I have the impression that they're not displeased. They're the first clients we've had who don't seem worried there aren't fourteen toilets to every floor. (*Turns back to the leading Japanese.*) Of course I imagine in Japan you daren't build anything like as substantially as this?

JAPANESE CLIENT I'm sorry?

WELBY (*with a pitying smile*) The earthquakes.

JAPANESE CLIENT Oh no. Office blocks in Japan much taller than this.

WELBY Really? Is that wise?

PHILLIPS We don't want to show them the top floor.

WELBY No, not if we can help it. (*turning to the clients*) Well, that's it, gentlemen.

JAPANESE CLIENT (*with papers*) No. No. There are nine floors. We have only seen eight floors.

Welby raises his eyebrows in despair to Phillips, but quickly turns it into another welcoming smile.

WELBY Quite right. Lead the way, George. I should explain the top floor is still pretty well in a state of nature . . .

The Japanese follow him out, with Phillips looking very glum and keeping in the rear.

INT. SUNLEY HOUSE: TOP FLOOR. DAY.

On the top floor Phillips keeps very much in the background, watching while Welby leads the Japanese round. Nearer and nearer the screen. Then away from the screen. The Japanese confer in the centre of the room. Now Welby takes the Japanese on to the gallery outside the building. He describes the view.

WELBY I'm glad we're seeing the top floor. It gives me an opportunity to show you the executive promenade. London, gentlemen. Flower of cities all. (*pointing out the landmarks*) Apex House. The Vickers Building. Our old friend the Post Office Tower.

The Japanese have noticed Rycroft asleep and are peeping through the glass at him. Phillips looks on aghast, while Welby waffles on.

It has been well said, gentlemen, that a man who is tired of London is tired of life.

He suddenly realises no one is listening, looks round, following the gaze of the astonished Japanese, and sees Rycroft fast asleep.

Good God! (*to Phillips*) Good God!

He rushes inside, pursued by the Japanese. They all gaze at the bedroll, etc., set out behind the screen. Rycroft's trousers over a chair. As they look, Rycroft sits up, unshaven.

WELBY Goodness gracious me. Rycroft? Rycroft.

PHILLIPS Rycroft?

WELBY It's Rycroft.

The Japanese crowd round, with wondering eager smiles.

JAPANESE CLIENT Lycloft? Lycloft?

RYCROFT Sir. I've been on guard . . . I'm on the lookout . . .
squatters . . .

WELBY Lookout? Squatters?

JAPANESE CLIENT (*alarmed*) Squatters?

WELBY Nonsense, gentlemen. We have no squatters. Not now,
Rycroft.

RYCROFT Sir.

WELBY Take no notice . . . I think we've seen all this floor has
to offer, gentlemen. As my colleague was saying, the view is
an enormous asset . . .

Rycroft comes across the room in his shirt tails.

RYCROFT Sir . . .

The Japanese laugh.

WELBY Please, Rycroft. Take no notice of the young man,
gentlemen . . . a precaution the insurance companies insist upon
in a building of this quality. A form of residential security . . .
my fault . . . I'd quite forgotten about him . . . Like Tolstoy,
servants sleeping across the threshold. Do you have Tolstoy in
Japan?

*He ushers them away. Behind the backs of the Japanese, Welby
raises his eyebrows to Phillips in despair as Rycroft stands in the
middle of the room calling after him.*

RYCROFT Sir . . . sir . . .

INT. FROBISHER, RENDELL & ROSS: OUTER OFFICE/PHILLIPS'S
OFFICE. DAY.

WELBY I could have been cross. I ought to have been cross.
I *wasn't* cross since it's obviously something mental, but those
Nips were on a knife edge. It could have gone either way.

PHILLIPS He's keen. He thought he was on to something.

WELBY A squatter, yes. I don't want to hear it, George.
Explanations. One felt so foolish. Is he us, George? We're really
a very old-fashioned firm. I don't think he's ever really
appreciated that. He had poor Peggy in tears only last week.
I don't like to see that. An employee of such long standing. No,
I think we probably ought to let him go. For his own sake.

PHILLIPS He's young. A little love nest probably.

WELBY Don't. He was babbling on about fingerprints. Fingerprints. As if the police don't have enough to do. And did you
notice, there was a *Bible* there. That's always a bad sign. Funny,
he didn't seem that type at all. Still, I think he'd be much
happier if we were to let him go. What a place to choose. Such
a prime location. You were quite right. Thought so all the time:
it had to wait its turn, find the right client. Glad it's Japs. So
reliable. Drink?

PHILLIPS I won't.

They go into the corridor.

INT. FROBISHER, RENDELL & ROSS: CORRIDOR. DAY.
*Out of vision, we hear Miss Venables and Mr Steele going through their
interminable list.*

MISS VENABLES Guildford, Jenner Road.

STEELE Guildford, Jenner Road.

MISS VENABLES Guildford, Warren Road.

STEELE Guildford, Warren Road.

MISS VENABLES EarIsfield, Marsham Street.

STEELE Earlsfield, Marsham Street.

MISS VENABLES 16 Bradshaw Place, SE9.

STEELE SE9, 16 Bradshaw Place.

MISS VENABLES 12 Lord North Street, SW1.

STEELE SW1, Lord North Street, Number 12.

MISS VENABLES 40 Smith Square, SW1.

STEELE Smith Square, SW1, Number 40.

MISS VENABLES 14 Chelsea Square.

STEELE 14 Chelsea Square.

And so on. Out of vision, we hear Blount discussing some deal.

BLOUNT Well try fifty-six. I don't hold out any hopes but try
fifty-six. They're an oldish couple, he's retiring, so they are going
to have to sell. Though whether they'll come down as much as
that I wouldn't like to say. No. To hell with it. Try fifty-six.

Then, out of vision, Blake and Marsh.

BLAKE So what's wrong with one-thirty?

MARSH There's a queue, that's what's wrong with it. One-thirty.
One-thirty is as bad as twelve-thirty.

BLAKE So when are we supposed to play the bloody game: two in
the morning?

MARSH What about *before* work? Eight-thirty?

BLAKE Eight-thirty! I'll be rising at dawn.

MARSH I'll get back to you.

BLAKE And remember twelve-thirty is favourite.

INT. FROBISHER, RENDELL & ROSS: OUTER OFFICE/PHILLIPS'S
OFFICE. DAY.

The secretaries going full blast.

AVRIL (*while phoning*) Went out with Vince and Pauline again last
night. Are you holding? They've found this pub where they do
proper Manhattans. Salt round the glass, everything. Did you
say three bedrooms?

SANDRA Salt?

AVRIL Northwood. The landlord used to work on a liner. Three
bedrooms, two reception, games room and granny flat, is that
the one? Forty-five thousand pounds.

*Phillips goes through to his office, and sits at his desk. Christine is on
the phone. She watches him while talking. His desk is still cleared, as
he left it the previous night.*

CHRISTINE Ten thousand square feet. On four floors. Yes. Loading
bay. Rear access and two minutes from the M4. Well, that
depends on the traffic, doesn't it? It says two minutes. Right.
I'll put it in the post, you'll have it in the morning. Goodbye.

Phillips is looking out of the window.

PHILLIPS I suppose there were always buildings here. It's a ford,
you see. Where they crossed the river. There'll always have
been some kind of settlement. (*He starts to put back his things
into the drawers.*)

INT. PHILLIPS'S HOME: LOUNGE. NIGHT.

*Phillips is in the lounge listening to music. Robin is there and Mrs
Phillips. Robin has a new girl, June. Phillips has headphones on again.
Mrs Phillips is reading. Robin stands up with June, seemingly
preparatory to going to bed. Phillips takes off headphones.*

PHILLIPS Darling, isn't it time Robin was taking June home?

MRS PHILLIPS Is it? I suppose it is.

ROBIN I think she's probably going to stay.

PHILLIPS It's after eleven. School tomorrow.

ROBIN Why? You've let me before.

June is in the background of this exchange but not in earshot.

PHILLIPS Yes. I don't know why. But I think she probably ought to go.

ROBIN Dad.

PHILLIPS No.

He stares the boy down.

MRS PHILLIPS You see, we're older than you.

Robin gives in and goes. Phillips looks almost regretful.

Fascinating, this book on lateral thinking.

PHILLIPS What?

MRS PHILLIPS I think I might try and find out more about it. Are you coming up?

PHILLIPS In a minute.

She goes. He sits.

Marks

CAST AND CREDITS

MARJORY	Marjorie Yates
LES	Ian Targett
DAD	Charles Lamb
LILY	Dandy Nichols
NORA	Diana Rayworth
LESLEY	Tracylynn Stephens
MARGARET	Colette Barker
PHOTOGRAPHER	Ojah Maharaj
VICAR	Nicholas Denney
DENISE	Frances Ruffell
A DAD	Sydney Golder
A MOTHER	Helen Keating
A BROTHER	Peter Acre
HUSBAND	John Fowler
BABY	Claire Cowell
Directed by	Piers Haggard
Designed by	Oliver Bayldon
Music by	Geoffrey Burgon

INT. CHURCH. DAY.

*A church. The font, where a baptism is taking place. The camera begins
with the sign of the cross being made on the head of a baby by a
youngish vicar with a beard.*

VICAR In the name of the Father, and of the Son and of the Holy
Ghost. Amen.

*The camera takes in the young parents, who are seventeen or eighteen.
The relatives of the young parents are gathered round the font in two
distinct groups: the relatives on the father's side, who are jolly, a bit
overdressed and have had a drink or two; and the young mother's
relatives, who stand a little apart – the girl's mother, Marjory, who is
about forty-five, her son Leslie, who is fifteen or sixteen, and another
woman, Nora, Marjory's friend. Marjory looks fed up, Leslie is
expressionless. Of the three of them, only Nora looks at all happy. Cut
to the end of the ceremony. The congregation is filing out, the young
mother, Margaret, carrying her baby. She pauses by her mother.*

MARGARET Happy? (*meaning 'Satisfied?'*)

*Marjory says nothing. She puts her arm through Leslie's, who looks
uncomfortable.*

EXT. CHURCH STEPS. DAY.

*A photographer is posing them all on the steps. Marjory is still
unsmiling. There is a definite sense that the family on the young father's
side is a bit common. Lots of banter.*

PHOTOGRAPHER Close in a bit.

FIRST VOICE Yes, budge up.

SECOND VOICE Give over, Denise.

THIRD VOICE Any closer and we shall be here again in nine
months' time.

FOURTH VOICE (*woman*) Wilfred!

SECOND VOICE I'm being assaulted here.

THIRD VOICE Change places with me then.

FOURTH VOICE You've clicked my stocking now, Wilfred, arsing
about.

FIRST VOICE Mind the bloody baby, I mean.

PHOTOGRAPHER Come on everybody. Lady in the blue hat, smile, love, please.

LES Come on, Mum. Crack one.

Marjory forces a smile.

THIRD VOICE (*whispered*) Hey. 'She gave a grim smile.'
Titters.

PHOTOGRAPHER One for the mantelpiece now.

EXT. TERRACE OF HOUSES. DAY.
Establishing shot.

INT. MARJORY'S HOME. DAY.
*Ordinary terrace house. Nora and Marjory talk, Nora has her hat
and coat on, so it is plainly not her house. Leslie has headphones on,
plugged in to a cassette recorder, and occasionally sings a phrase or two
in a toneless unintelligible way.*

NORA It was you wanted her christening.

MARJORY Not with a name like that.

NORA It's a nice name.

MARJORY Kimberley? Kimberley? It's the name of a place.

NORA No, that's Camberley.

MARJORY Kimberley. It's in Australia. It's where that diamond came from.

NORA Well, she is a little jewel.

MARJORY Saddled with a name like that. She's marked for life. She's no taste, Margaret. She takes after her dad. Kimberley.
Les takes his earphones off for a second.

LES I like it.

MARJORY What?

LES Kimberley.

NORA Give us a listen. (*She puts on the earphones and listens happily, saying, in a too-loud voice:*) Turn it down.

MARJORY He ought to have put her off it, that vicar. Advised her. You'd never think he was a vicar outside. One of these 'We're just the same as you are' brigade. Only I bet his daughter's not called Kimberley. She'll by Polly. Or Jane. Proper names. I just wanted her called Susan. Something ordinary.
Nora takes them off.

NORA It's like you're somewhere else.

LES Try it.

Marjory shakes her head.

Live a bit.

MARJORY How? I'm a grandmother. Imagine calling her in on a night. Kimberley! Kimberley!

Les has got his earphones on again.

NORA You've still got one (*meaning Les*).

MARJORY Yes. Margaret was always a big Dad fan anyway. I don't know what he's going to do.

They are free to talk about Les because he has his earphones on and is oblivious.

Schools, they do it on you. He's had satisfactory reports all the way through. Marks good. 'Does well.' 'Up to standard.' I knew he couldn't spell, but I thought, 'Well, the school will know' compared with the average. Then the letter comes. Failed everything. CSEs. Whole bloody lot. Not even graded. I go down there and his teacher says they never expected him to pass. I said to him 'So what does "up to standard" mean?' And he says, 'Well, you know, he's a nice enough lad.' What's that got to do with it? It's a fraud, schooling now. If they're clever they keep them back. If they're not they pretend they are. Nobody lays it down. Then it's too late. I could spell.

NORA You write a grand letter, you always have.

MARJORY Sums. All that.

NORA They have these calculators now. Still, he's lovely-looking. And he's shy. I always think that's nice.

INT. KITCHEN. DAY.

Marjory and Les are washing up. Nora has gone.

MARJORY Seventeen.

LES Don't keep saying seventeen. You just don't like being a grandmother.

MARJORY Promise me you won't ever get yourself into that boat with a girl.

Les reaches for his headphones. She stops him.

Promise me.

LES Mum. Girls don't like me. I don't say the right things.

MARJORY If it's what he said to Margaret, good job. And any girl that doesn't like you wants her head examining. You're lovely.

She touches him. He pulls away.

LES It's the girl's responsibility now, anyway.

MARJORY What?

LES Birth control.

MARJORY You seem to know a lot about it.

LES We did it at school. (*He puts the headphones on.*)

MARJORY School. They get that into your heads. You can't
spell, but you know all about birth control. Birth control's not
going to get you a job. You can't say that at your interview.
'What qualifications have you?' 'I know about birth control.'
Margaret can't even say that. She must have been looking out
of the window. (*She looks at herself in the mirror.*) Forty-three.

LES What?

MARJORY I'm a grandmother.

LES Well *she* was, that German bag. And she did all right.

MARJORY What German bag?

LES I don't know. That German bag. With the nice legs. Maureen
somebody.

MARJORY Maureen? Maureen? *Marlene.* Marlene Dietrich.
Maureen Dietrich. How are you ever going to get a job, you
don't even know Marlene Dietrich.
They both laugh.

INT. KITCHEN. DAY.

Marjory is ready to go to work. Les is having his breakfast.

MARJORY Do you read any newspapers?

LES No.

MARJORY I'm testing you.

LES The *Sun.*

MARJORY Say the *Mail.* The *Mail*'s better. It's classier.

LES Today's only a formality, Mam. He's not going to give me
a job. He'll just put me down on the register.

MARJORY You don't know what tips the balance. What do you do
in your spare time?

LES It's all spare time.

MARJORY Say you were in full employment.
Les studies.
Try, Les.
Nothing.

You listen to music, don't you?

LES I listen to music.

MARJORY Pop or classical?

LES Rock.

MARJORY Say some classical.

LES What if he asks what?

MARJORY Say . . . say Tchaikovsky. You've got to push yourself,
Les. You can't just trot out the Top Twenty. They'll all do that.
Show you're different.

LES I'm not different.

MARJORY Isn't there some respectable pop now? Serious. Elvis
Presley's serious, isn't he, now he's dead? We used to like
Buddy Holly. Hasn't he come round again?

LES It'll just be somebody that takes your name down.

MARJORY But you don't seem to know anything.

LES You don't know anything. It doesn't matter.

MARJORY Something matters. Something's got to matter. (*getting
a bit of paper out of her bag*) Promise me something?

LES What?

MARJORY Don't go in your jeans. (*She reads the scrap of paper.*)
I cut this out at work:
'When to an interview you do go
Dress carefully, but without show,
Arrive on time, don't chew or smoke
Or else they'll choose the other bloke.'
It has no noticeable effect on Les.
I think you should look in these newsagents' shop windows.
Cards. That's where the jobs are. At grass roots level. Give us a
kiss. (*She is just going when she stops.*) And if you have to fill in
any forms, your father's dead.
Les says nothing.
Do you hear? Dead.

LES He's not dead. He's living in Bristol.

MARJORY Your father is dead.

She goes. He reaches for the earphones.

INT. HOUSE. DAY.
*Montage of Les doing housework with earphones on. Hoovering,
emptying ashtrays, washing up.*

EXT. JOB CENTRE.
Establishing shot.

INT. JOB CENTRE. DAY.
*A youngish, bearded man at a desk interviewing Les. They are in a
cubicle closed on three sides. In another cubicle sits another interviewer.
One should be able to see both interviewers in the same shot if need be.
Though they cannot see one another.*

BEARD Hang-gliding? *Hang-gliding?* Cost you, hang gliding.
    Where do you get the money to go hang gliding?

LES I sometimes go to watch.

BEARD (*wearily*) Then it's not a hobby, is it? Spectating is not a
    hobby. (*He raises his voice, addressing Des in the other cubicle.*)
    It's like sport, Des, all these jokers, you ask them for a hobby
    and they say football. Only they don't play. Doing, lad, that's
    what we're after. Doing. Not watching. (*He writes something
    down.*) What gives, Des?
    Des is sitting in his cubicle staring into space.

DES As of now, Dave, nothing. A slight hiccup in the
    never-ending procession of square pegs desirous of being
    inserted into round holes.
    Les sits expressionless throughout this.

BEARD All right for some. (*There is a thick folder and a thin folder
    on his desk.*) Jobs required. Jobs available. We're in a loaves and
    fishes situation here. Do you fancy being a lavatory attendant?

LES No.

BEARD Private Secretary to a Nobel Prizewinner?

LES N–no.

BEARD Right, well, we've established the parameters. (*Pause while
    he looks at Les's form.*) Aren't you interested in anything?

LES I'd like to travel.

BEARD Louder. I didn't hear.

LES (*louder*) I'd like to travel.
    *Beard lifts his hand, as if giving a cue and promptly Des, without
    amusement or interest says:*

DES What in?

BEARD Why do you want to travel?
    Leslie says nothing.

LES Broadens the mind.

BEARD I travel, don't I, Des?

Des says nothing. They have obviously done this routine many times.

Every day between here and Fordyce Road. Never broadens mine.

At which point the office door opens and a pretty but expressionless girl comes in with two coffees and biscuits for Beard and the other man.

All hail, Christine. It is the hour of custard creams.

CHRISTINE Fig rolls.

BEARD You have a nice bum, Christine.

Christine looks used to this.

It is the only thing that keeps me going, is your bum. Faced with a character with no O Levels, no CSEs, no ideas and no ambitions, I think, 'Well we have always Christine's bum.' When you get a job . . . What's your name . . . Leslie. (*He looks at Les's form.*) . . . If you get a job, whether you are digging a septic tank or are Personal Assistant to the head of the CBI, job satisfaction will not consist in any work that you are employed to do. It will consist in incidentals. Like Christine's bum.

LES And Maureen's tits.

BEARD Goodbye, bum.

Christine goes out, unmoved.

LES I wondered about the Army.

BEARD Ever feel you've been here before, Des?

He reaches behind him without looking and takes a leaflet from the rack behind him. There is silence in the office. Les looking at the Army form. Beard bored. Other man staring into space.

INT. MARJORY'S LIVING ROOM. DAY.

Les is in his underpants, ironing a shirt.

MARJORY You have got skills. Ironing's a skill. Hoovering's a skill. Looking after the house, that's a skill. Look at your dad. He couldn't make a cup of tea.

Les goes on ironing.

You could be a butler. A gentleman's gentleman. All that's at your fingertips.

He goes on ironing. She watches him.

You're a lovely-looking lad, Les. The one that gets you is going to be lucky.

He doesn't look at her, but says:

LES Don't, Mum.

MARJORY Don't what?

LES Don't look at me.

MARJORY I'm your mum. I'm allowed to look at you.

LES You want to find yourself a chap. (*He puts on the shirt he has been ironing.*)

MARJORY I don't want a chap. Even part-time. What do I want with a chap? I had a chap. I had my bellyfull with a chap. Twice.

LES Your life's not over.

MARJORY That part of it is.

LES There'd be some fellers jump at you. (*He goes upstairs.*)

MARJORY (*calling after him*) Bring your jeans down and I'll wash them.

INT. LES'S BEDROOM. DAY.

Les is ready to go out. He gets out a small printing outfit with four or five different stamps. He carefully stamps a star on his palm. A square on the back. Another two signs on his left hand. Tries them out. Bunching his fist, the sign showing. It should be plain what he is doing, but not what he is doing it for.

INT. LIVING ROOM AND HALL. DAY.

MARJORY Your jeans.

LES They're upstairs.

She kisses him. The lipstick leaves a mark.

MARJORY I've lipsticked you.

She rubs it out.

LES Mum!

Marjory shrugs. Les goes. She irons a wrinkled shirt, then goes to the mirror and smooths out the unironable wrinkles on her neck; then goes upstairs.

INT. LES'S BEDROOM. DAY.

Marjory puts one or two items straight in his bedroom, then picks up his jeans. She takes a handkerchief out of the pocket, some coppers, which she puts on the mantelpiece. In the back pocket are the leaflets about the Army from the Job Centre. She sits down on the bed looking at them.

INT./EXT. SCHOOL ENTRANCE AND PLAYGROUND. EARLY EVENING.

From inside, the sounds of disco music. At the door, a man is taking money as kids go in. Two girls come out, one with a boy. The man stamps their hands for a pass-out.

SECOND GIRL (*to First Girl*) Don't be long.

The boy gives a dirty laugh as they go off together. Second Girl is left.

Possibly the whole of this scene could be played on roller skates. Second Girl skating disconsolately round the yard. Les eyes the girl for a bit.

LES Hey.

SECOND GIRL What?

LES Can I look at your stamp?

She looks at him, but says nothing.

Can I look at your stamp?

SECOND GIRL What for?

LES I just want to see it.

SECOND GIRL What for?

LES Go on. Show us.

SECOND GIRL Do I know you?

LES Is it like this?

He shows her his hand, which she looks at without interest.

SECOND GIRL No.

LES This?

Showing her another mark.

SECOND GIRL Could be.

LES That?

SECOND GIRL No.

LES That?

SECOND GIRL (*pityingly*) No.

LES (*certain*) That?

The girl's face changes.

SECOND GIRL No.

LES It is.

SECOND GIRL It isn't.

LES Show us then – go on. (*He makes grab for her wrist.*)

SECOND GIRL Leave off, you.

She shows him her hand. It has a mark stamped on it like one of his.

SECOND GIRL I could report you. (*She is looking at the Chucker Out.*) He's merciless, is that one. I know his sister. He has a caravan and an Alsatian dog. It's not fair on other people. Let's have another look. It's uncanny. Would you do it for me? Say I got to know you?

LES If you want.

SECOND GIRL I was supposed to make a useful contact today. It said in my horoscope.

LES Here goes.

They go in. The Chucker Out scarcely glances at the mark.

SECOND GIRL Jammy bugger.

LES (*disappointed*) He never even looked. (*She takes Les's hand.*) I don't dance.

SECOND GIRL What you come in for?

LES Watch.

EXT. TERRACE OF HOUSES. DUSK.

LES You can't come in.

SECOND GIRL I don't want to come in. Why?

LES My mum.

SECOND GIRL She poorly?

LES No. Narrow-minded.

SECOND GIRL Mine isn't. She's got a chap. Come in there.

LES Where do you live?

SECOND GIRL Crossfields.

LES I'm not trailing all that way.

SECOND GIRL Well, I've got to.

LES You can come round tomorrow. In the daytime. She goes out to work.

SECOND GIRL In the daytime? What for?

LES How do you mean, what for?

SECOND GIRL What do you want me to come round for?

LES I don't, particularly.

SECOND GIRL What time?

LES Any time.

She is going.

SECOND GIRL You never asked me my name.

LES It'll keep.

He is going in. Marjory is sitting at the table. She has the Army brochures in front of her.

INT. MARJORY'S BEDROOM. MORNING.

Les comes into his mother's bedroom in his pyjama trousers and a shirt with a cup of tea. Marjory is in bed facing away from him.

LES Mum, Mum. I've brought you some tea, Mum.

MARJORY (*not turning round*) What's the time?

LES After half past.

She turns round, unsmiling, and takes the tea.

Mum?

MARJORY What?

LES They were only leaflets. I didn't sign anything.

MARJORY Do what you want. Go back to bed.

Marjory starts to get up. Les waits for a moment.

LES Mum?

Marjory won't speak.

INT. LES'S BEDROOM. MORNING.

He is lying in bed. He hears the door bang as she goes to work. Looks at the clock. Gets up.

INT. SITTING ROOM. MORNING.

Les is tidying the room up, headphones on.

INT. LES'S BEDROOM. MORNING.

He looks at the sheets; switches them round. He has just finished when the bell goes downstairs. He gives the bedroom a last look.

EXT. TERRACE. DAY.

Marjory and Nora walking home.

MARJORY Shortfall. What's shortfall got to do with us? We're canteen. Canteen can't have a shortfall. It's wicked. No notice. Nothing.

NORA It's better than being finished. Three days a week is better than being finished.

MARJORY I can't see how we're going to manage. Are you coming in?
She does.

INT. KITCHEN AND LIVING ROOM. DAY.
Les is in the kitchen in his shirt filling the kettle. Marjory and Nora's arrival startles him.
LES Jesus. What's matter?
MARJORY Just getting up? I thought you were going round newsagents' windows. What's matter?
LES Nothing. What are you doing home?
MARJORY Sacked.
NORA We haven't been sacked. We're on short time.
MARJORY Then you'd have to find a job, if I was sacked. What's *matter?*
LES Nothing.
MARJORY What've you been doing? (*She finds a coat on the settee.*) Whose is this?
Les goes upstairs quickly and without speaking. Marjory calls up after him.
Les. Leslie.
Marjory, holding the coat, looks at Nora.
NORA I'll go. (*She is going.*) It's normal nowadays.
Nora goes. Les comes down with his trousers on.
MARJORY So this is what you do, is it?
LES No.
MARJORY No wonder you're not busting to find a job if this is what you do.
LES I don't.
MARJORY You don't? You do.
LES It's the first time.
MARJORY I don't want to know. Just get her out of the house. Who is she?
LES She's nobody.
The girl has appeared in the doorway.
I just met her last night.
MARJORY I thought you were the shy one. I thought you were the one couldn't talk to girls.
LES I can't.

MARJORY I suppose you haven't had much talking to do.
(*Marjory catches sight of her, stood in the doorway.*) What's your
name?

GIRL Lesley.

MARJORY Your name, not his name.

LES Her name's Lesley.

MARJORY His name's Leslie.

GIRL Yes.

MARJORY That's disgusting.

GIRL It's spelled different.

MARJORY I don't care how it's spelled. What the hell difference
does it make how you spell it? And what were you doing?
How's that spelled?

GIRL I didn't want to come here. We could have gone up home.
My mum doesn't mind.

MARJORY Well she bloody well ought to mind. How old are you?

GIRL Fourteen?

MARJORY Fourteen. (*She starts to cry.*)

LES Mum.

GIRL I'll go. It's funny. My mum never turns a hair.
She goes.

LES Mum.

MARJORY Go after her. She's your girl.

LES She isn't.

MARJORY You've been to bed with her. Go after her. What do
you think she feels like?

LES She won't mind. I didn't even like her.

MARJORY You should like her. That's what it reckons to be about.

LES Not these days.

MARJORY You haven't even got started. You haven't even found
your feet and you're off on that game. You're never going to get
anywhere now. It makes up for everything, does that.

LES What?

MARJORY That. And drink. It's why nobody gets anywhere. Same
as Margaret. You start on that game, you wake up one
morning, you're thirty-five, you've got two kids and you're
nowhere. You want to get somewhere before you start fetching
girls home.

LES You can't do stuff in order. I might not have a job for years.

MARJORY You haven't looked. I tell you. Go round knocking on doors. Looking at adverts.

LES All right. I'll go this afternoon. But I know it's no good.
Pause.

MARJORY Funny her having your name. Is that how you got talking?

LES No. I only asked her name when we got upstairs. It put me right off. Lesley.

MARJORY It's a nice name. In a boy. She wasn't a patch on you anyway. Fetch your sheets down. I'll wash them.
He goes for his headphones.
Did you do that in headphones?
He grins.
I expect they will be doing before long.

EXT. STREET. DAY.
Les looking in shop windows at cards. (Say two shots.) He looks closer at one card and copies down an address.

EXT. COUNCIL ESTATE. DAY.
Les approaching a concrete council block. He climbs a staircase. We see him ring a doorbell. A woman of about sixty opens it. We see her shake her head before beginning to hear the conversation.

LILY No. Not here.

LES Fifty-five.

LILY I don't care. It's not here.
While she is talking to him she is looking behind him and around to make sure no one is watching.

LILY No.

DAD (*from behind the door*) What's he look like?
Lily is still casing the landing and stairs.

LILY Youngish. Sixteen. Are you genuine?
Les is puzzled.

LES What?

LILY Come in.

DAD (*behind door*) Sharp.

INT. FLAT. DAY.
Lily pushes door open, and they bundle Les inside. Dad is older than Lily and more frail.

LILY Now then. Where did you find the address?

LES In a window.

DAD Which window?

LES Down Lorrimer Road.

DAD It is down Lorrimer Road.

LILY I don't know. What do you think, Dad?

Dad has been running his hand over Les's arm. There is a tattoo on Dad's hand.

LES You've got a tattoo.

DAD I've got a tattoo, yes.

LILY What does that prove? Doesn't prove it's a tattooist's, does it? A tattooist's'd have pictures on the wall. Designs. There'd be machines, needles. Paraphernalia. This is just an ordinary home.

DAD He's got an earring.

LILY Earrings don't mean nothing. They all have earrings. Police have earrings.

LES They don't.

DAD He's only young.

LILY That might be part of it.

LES I'm off.

DAD Why?

LES I've changed my mind.

DAD Supposing I did them, what sort of tattoo were you thinking of.

LES 'Mother'. Just 'Mother'.

DAD Whereabouts?

LES My arm.

Pause.

DAD He's not from the Council. You're not from the Council. They don't wear earrings on the Council.

LES Why should I be from the Council?

LILY Rates. We're domestic rated. Council finds out he's running a business, they could have us out.

DAD I'm not running a business. I do it more as a favour. One here, one there.

LILY Feller on the end, started selling tropical fish from his front room. Just odd ones, now and again, to bona fide fish fanciers. Six o'clock one morning, knock on the door. Out. Fish tanks stuck on the pavement. Heartbroken. And she was just getting over shingles.

DAD Take your coat off.

LILY Take your coat off. He did have premises once upon a time.

DAD Up till two years ago.

LILY Two years ago. On Station Street. He was famous wherever tattooed people foregathered. Signed photographs in the window. Johnny Ray, Frankie Vaughan. Only he's had one or two setbacks health-wise.

DAD I had a stroke.

LILY You didn't have a stroke. Not a full-blown stroke. His speech was affected. Nothing else. I'll never be convinced it was a stroke. And even his speech wasn't bad. I could always understand, couldn't I, Dad? No, you're in safe hands here.
But Dad has a definite tremor in his hands.
Lifetime of experience.

DAD Get my book down.

LILY I'll get your book down.
She opens a cupboard and takes out a big book carefully wrapped up. Old and battered, it is his book of designs.
This is the Bible.
Dad smiles.
And it was 'Mother'?

LES Yes.

DAD There's lots of Mothers. There's half-a-dozen Mothers. Show him Mothers, Lily.
She is turning over the pages.
Flags, Jesus, Mary, Mermaids. Give it here, Lily. (*He takes it.*)

LILY No, Dad, you've passed Mothers.
Dad has some difficulty separating the pages because of his tremor.
There, see. You glance at those while I take out his equipment. He can be glancing at those while I take out your equipment.
Les looks at them.

DAD We'll want a clean cloth, Lily.

LILY Oh yes. A clean cloth. (*Lily gets out a tray cloth and spreads it on the table.*) Came from Hong Kong, this cloth. He was always very particular. That parlour in Station Street, it was spotless. It's clinical, tattooing. It's like a surgical operation.

DAD It doesn't hurt.

LILY I didn't mean it hurt. I meant from a hygiene point of view.
It's like a surgical operation from a hygiene point of view.
DAD Shut up. Talking about operations. You'll frighten the client.
LILY You're not frightened, are you?
LES No.
LILY He's not frightened, Dad. The client's not frightened. (*Lily
takes out a box.*) These are his needles. They have to be
sterilised. I boil them up in a bit of Dettol, personally. It's the
boiling that does it. The Dettol's optional.
*She takes them into the kitchen, puts them in a pan and pours some
water from a kettle over them, then switches the gas on. While she is
waiting for them to boil, Dad comes in, opens the kitchen cupboard,
and takes a nip from a bottle of whisky. She tactfully ignores this.
She eats a bit of chicken from a Kentucky Fried Chicken box.*
I'm eating this bit of chicken.
Les sits in the living room, waiting. He is uneasy. Dad comes back.
DAD I generally let her do the preparations. Marriage, you help
each other. Have you chosen?
LES I think I'll have this one.
DAD Oh yes. I like that one. That's one of the ones I like.
LILY You chosen? Oh yes. I like that one. He'll do you a
beautiful job on that one, you'll see. (*She takes the shade off an
ordinary table lamp and puts it on the table, having first of all
drawn the curtains, and looked out.*) 'All clear.' This was a
wedding present, this –
*She goes out again. The cloth is spread on the table. The lamp is
by it. It should look almost like a mass. Lily comes back with the
needle.*
DAD Do you want it on your forearm?
LES I think so.
DAD Not your bicep?
LES No. My arm.
LILY I thought forearm. Since it's his first. Shouldn't run before
you can walk.
DAD Shut up, Lily, and give me the razor.
*Lily hands Dad the razor, a cut-throat, while she puts some lather
on Les's arm with a stubby shaving brush. Dad's hand is noticeably
shaking as it holds the razor.*
LILY I could do the shaving, if you want.

DAD I don't want.

LILY Naught much to shave really.

DAD It has to be smooth.

LILY Oh yes, it has to be smooth. Only it is smooth. I don't like a man with too much hair.

Dad finishes the shaving.

DAD Beautiful.

LILY Beautiful.

Dad now applies a transfer of the design to Les's arm. He is about to start.

DAD It might just hurt a bit to start with.

LILY Just a bit to start with.

DAD It's only like a tingling.

LILY A tingling.

DAD Shut up, Lily. (*He is about to start.*)

LILY Dad.

DAD What?

LILY Disinfectant, Dad.

DAD Oh ay. It's you, you know, going on. You're putting me off. I never had her down at Station Street. (*He swabs the arm with some stuff from a little bottle.*) Here we go. (*Dad starts the needle, and puts it on Les's arm.*)

LES (*at the pain*) Oh, *Mother.*

DAD Steady as she blows.

LES Jesus.

Dad tattoos in silence for a bit.

LILY There you are, Dad, you see. It's all right. (*She smiles at Les.*) The boy's more nervous than you are.

DAD (*suddenly angry*) Go next door, woman. It's not for you, this. It's a man's job, this.

She goes out and sits in the kitchen. Camera stays with her in the kitchen, sitting listening to the sound of the tattooing.

LILY (*calling*) All right?

DAD All right. Flesh has textures, you know. It can be like paper, it can be like cloth. The grain is different. This is a fine skin. It's like a girl's.

Les watching Dad tattooing his arm.

LILY (*calling out*) You can talk and do it, Dad, you see. I told you.

DAD Take no notice. You'd be surprised at the people that has
     tattoos. Film stars. Trade union leaders. Royalty. The Prince of
     Wales had one.
LES Which one?
DAD Which Prince of Wales, Lily?
LILY (*calling*) Him that died.
DAD A man that has a tattoo is a free man. He's someone that's
     taken a decision. All the rest of you is what you got given.
     Got from your parents. You take after your mother or you take
     after your father. But this, this is you, setting your mark upon
     yourself. You're grown up now. A man.
     In the kitchen, Lily blows her nose.

INT. MARJORY'S HOME. DAY.
*Marjory is ironing the sleeve of one of Les's white shirts. She finishes,
puts it on a hanger and hangs it up, smiling slightly. She runs her hand
down the sleeve of the clean, white shirt. She looks happy.*

INT. FLAT. DAY.
A little later. The sound of the tattooing needle stops.
DAD Lily.
LILY What?
DAD It's done.
     Lily comes into the room with some tea.
LILY There. I knew it would be all right. Doesn't that look
     lovely? Once it's healed up it'll be something to be proud of,
     and a real talking point.
LES I didn't tell my mum.
LILY Well, she can't complain about that, can she? Mother. You
     must be fond of her.
LES Yes.
LILY I like a boy that's fond of his mother.
DAD It's quite usual.
LILY Not these days.
DAD It's one of the ones I used to get asked for most often.
LILY Not 'Father', though. I don't think I've ever seen anybody
     with 'Father' tattooed on him.
DAD No. I've never had to do 'Father'. But 'Mother' – oh, every
     day of the week.

LILY Show him mine, Dad.

Dad rolls his sleeve up and shows him 'Lily' tattooed on his arm.
That was done before we were married. I'll put you some stuff
on it.

DAD I'll do it.

LILY No holding him now, is there!

DAD It's an art form, is this. They've woken up to that in America.

LILY America. And Japan.

DAD And Japan. Not in the UK.

LILY Dragging our footsteps as usual.

DAD But remember, if you ever want to start an interesting
conversation, fetch it round to tattoos. (*He binds up Les's arm.*)

LILY It's coming back into fashion again. It tailed off a bit after
the war, but it's due for a boom. (*Lily helps Les carefully on with
his jacket.*) Course the rundown of the armed services hasn't
helped.

LES I might go in the Army.

DAD Oh well. This'll stand you in good stead there, this. Give you
some status with your mates. Marks you out, straightaway.

LES How much do I owe you?

DAD How much, Lily?

LILY Well, now then.

DAD It used to be five pounds, did that.

LILY But the cost of raw materials have gone up. And electric's
wicked.

DAD Still, I think five. For old times' sake. And you're only a boy.

LILY He thought you were from the Council.

They laugh. Les goes. They sit for a moment or two.

DAD Nice lad.

LILY Lovely.

DAD I never shook once, did you notice? Soon as I got hold of
the needle I never shook once.

LILY I knew.

DAD Steady as a rock.

LILY It's not been a stroke. I told you.

DAD Shaking now, though. Look. There's something not right.

LILY But you haven't lost the knack, that's the main thing.

She holds his shaking hand.

EXT. LANDING OF COUNCIL FLAT. DAY.
*Les going home. Tentatively feeling his arm. He shouldn't look
apprehensive: simply that he has a secret.*

INT. MARJORY'S. DAY.
Les is eating a meal with his fork in his right hand. Marjory not eating.

MARJORY Maybe we're attacking this from the wrong angle.
    I don't want to go on working at the canteen all my life.
    And we both get on. I wondered, if I could scrape up a bit
    of money . . .

LES What?

MARJORY Personalised catering. In the City. Boardrooms.
    Functions. Business lunches, where they finalise deals. I could
    cook and you do the waiting.

LES Me a waiter?

MARJORY It's not complicated. You'd want a white coat. Some
    black trousers.

LES (*eagerly*) I've got some black trousers.

MARJORY That's right. We're halfway there. And it's simply a
    case of saying, 'Red or white?' Though some people now prefer
    a soft drink, the trend is away from alcohol, I was reading.

LES What would they eat?

MARJORY Salads with raisins. Quiches. It's every week in these
    magazines. Just fork things. We could, Leslie.

LES Yes? (*He is having difficulty eating something with just his fork.*)

MARJORY Use your knife, love. And once we'd done one or two
    and the word got round, it would snowball. Cut it up.

LES Do you reckon?

MARJORY *Yes.* What's the matter with your hand?

LES Nothing. When? When could we start?

MARJORY We'd have to go into it all very carefully. I can get a
    book out of the library. Oh, Les, just think. Is it sore?

LES No. What else could they eat?

MARJORY Sausages. Little, refined ones. Eggs scooped out.
    You've not been in a fight?

LES *No.* What else?

MARJORY Vol au vents. Does it hurt?

LES What's that?

MARJORY Little tarty things with stuff in. It is sore.

LES No. What else?

They are both now enthusiastic.

MARJORY Well, anything.

LES Could we do it? Just the two of us?

MARJORY Yes, I'm sure we could. Honestly.

She takes hold of him and he cries out.

MARJORY What's up? What have you done?

LES Nothing.

MARJORY Have you hurt yourself?

LES Mum. I'm having my tea.

MARJORY Roll your shirt up.

LES Mum, it's nothing.

She goes into the scullery. As soon as she is out of the room he eats with a fork in his right hand.

I met two nice people today.

MARJORY (*in the kitchen*) Where?

LES When I was going round. A couple. Old. Husband and wife. They kept a newsagents. He hadn't been well. She was helping out. He's had a stroke. What is a stroke?

MARJORY (*coming back*) Why?

LES This old man had had one.

MARJORY What old man?

LES I'm telling you.

MARJORY Les.

LES What?

MARJORY You're not still thinking about the Army.

LES No.

MARJORY You've not been getting yourself vaccinated?

LES *No.* I want to tell you about this couple. Listen to me about this couple. This husband and wife.

MARJORY I'm not interested in husbands and wives.

LES Tell me about catering.

Pause.

MARJORY No. What have you done?

LES You're *terrible*. It's a present. Only it's not ready yet.

MARJORY A present. You've hurt your arm. How can it be a present?

LES Turn around. And promise not to say anything. Because it's not right yet. (*He takes off the gauze pad.*) All right.

MARJORY Leslie!

LES It won't look like this. It's with it just having been done.

MARJORY *Leslie.*

LES He's given me the name of some stuff to put on. Can you see what it says?

MARJORY Les.

LES 'Mother.'

MARJORY You stupid little fool. You silly, stupid barmy little sod. What have you done?

LES I haven't done anything. I did it for you.

MARJORY For me? But there was no need to do anything for me. You were lovely. You were perfect. You didn't have to do anything for me. You were mine as you were. You were perfect. Now you're not perfect.

LES If all that makes me not perfect is having your name on my arm I don't mind. What will we call this firm?

MARJORY What firm?

LES Our firm.

MARJORY You little fool.

He tries to get hold of her.

Get off me. My name. It's not my name. You don't call me Mother. You call me Mum.

LES I thought 'Mother' was more classy. You're always wanting to be classy.

MARJORY You don't understand a thing, do you? Not a bloody thing. Did you really think I'd be pleased? Did you honestly think so? 'Mother.' That's not me. That's him. Father. That's what that says. Not Mother: Father. He had a tattoo. That's the kind of man he was.

LES Mum, it *hurts*. It hurts me now.

MARJORY It hurts *me*. It'll never come off. You're stuck with it. It's indelible, is that. It's like a bruise. A bloody great ornamental bruise. It's like my varicose veins, that blue. Is that what you wanted?

LES It isn't.

MARJORY Writing on your body. You can't even spell and you go writing on your body.

LES Lots of lads have them.

MARJORY Lads. Your dad used to talk about lads. Me and the lads. You've never been one of the lads. I hate the lads.

Marjory sits down and starts smoking. Les goes upstairs. She gets up and shouts up the stairs.

You'll never be able to take your clothes off in front of better-class people. (*She is coming back, then goes back to foot of the stairs.*) Who did it? Did he know how old you were? He wants reporting.

Les angry and at the top of the stairs.

LES They were nice.

MARJORY He ought to be ashamed of himself.

She is going back to the fireplace when she suddenly rushes upstairs into his bedroom.

INT. BEDROOM. DAY.

MARJORY I'll show you something. I'll show you my marks. (*She pulls up her skirt and pulls down her knickers.*) These. Do you see these marks. Stretch marks. You made them. That's your tattoo on me. You and Margaret.

LES Mum, I don't want to see you. I don't want to see you.

MARJORY Look.

INT. LIVING ROOM.

Les runs downstairs. Puts on his headphones and sits by the fire. Marjory follows him down after a moment or two.

MARJORY I'll tell you one thing. You'll never get a job now. Except a labouring job. And it's no good hiding your head in that stuff. Music. That won't get you anywhere. It's the same as sex: you're no further on when it stops. You're ruined, you. Finished.

He can't hear, but he says very loud because of the headphones:

LES Shut up.

MARJORY (*shouting*) Finished, you. Done for. (*She snatches the headphones off.*) Finished. Finished before you've even started. (*She chucks them in the fire. Or breaks them.*)

LES You stupid cow. You silly stupid cow.

Les hits Marjory in the face.

Oh, hell.

MARJORY You'll have marked me now.

LES Bathe it. Come on.

MARJORY Bathe that thing too. (*She gets a bowl and puts in on the table. She is smoking.*)

LES You shouldn't smoke, Mam.

MARJORY You make me smoke.

LES Here. Let's see.

Marjory lifts her face to the light and he bathes it. She wipes it with a towel.

MARJORY Maybe we could have it removed. I could save up maybe. They have skin grafts.

Camera should pull away from them both during this.

INT. A DARK ROOM.

A man (unfeatured) lying naked on his front on a bed. He is Les, older.

VOICE OVER But he never did have it removed. And in years to come when he looked at the tattoo it did always remind him of his mother, though not in the way it had been meant to. He remembered only her anger and her grief, and how she had wept to see him spoiled. It that sense the tattoo had served its purpose. It was a badge, an emblem. A mark that he was hers. It was as if she had engraved it herself.

A male hand strokes the tattoo.

A MALE VOICE Oh. You've got a tattoo. Tattoos always turn me on.

Say Something Happened

CAST AND CREDITS

MAM	Thora Hird
DAD	Hugh Lloyd
JUNE POTTER	Julie Walters

Directed by	Giles Foster
Designed by	Austin Ruddy
Music by	George Fenton

INT. LIVING ROOM. DAY.

The living room of a semi-detached house. A couple in their sixties are sitting there, the man in an easy chair, the woman gazing out of the window. Pause.

MAM More leaves coming down. (*Pause.*) Straight on to our path. (*Pause.*) I could be in and out all day. (*Pause.*) It's not right. It's her tree, yet somehow they're our leaves.

DAD I might get down the atlas in a minute. (*Pause.*) Try and spot Helsinki.

MAM I'm just wondering if I ought to wash one or two stockings. Don't upset.

Dad is getting up to get the atlas.

I've just this minute sat down. (*Pause.*) I shouldn't know where to look.

DAD Helsinki? Oh yes. It's the capital of Finland. It was a station on the little wireless we had when we were first married. Hilversum. Helsinki. Droitwich. No end of different places.

MAM All radio this that and the other now.

DAD It won't be so warm. Getting on for the Arctic Circle.

MAM It's to be hoped she takes them little bootee things we bought her. They'll be just what the doctor ordered in the Arctic Circle.

Dad is turning over the pages of the atlas.

DAD It can't be so far off Russia.

MAM (*alarmed*) Russia?

DAD She's a sensible girl. Russia won't worry our Margaret. (*He reads out the statistics from the atlas.*) 'Helsinki. Seaport and capital city of Finland. Population 2.7 million. Chief industries: carpets, sugar, paper-making . . .

The door chimes go.

. . . fisheries.'

MAM I hope this isn't next door. (*She stands up and looks out of the window.*) It's a young woman.

DAD What sort of a young woman?

MAM Educated. Got a briefcase. You go. Only, Dad . . .
Dad has got up and is going out into the hall. He pauses.
Put the chain on.
In the hall Dad puts the chain on and opens the door. We don't see the young woman.

DAD Hello.

JUNE Mr Rhodes?

DAD Yes.

JUNE June Potter. I'm from the Council. The Social Services Department.

DAD Yes?

JUNE You had a leaflet.

DAD What leaflet?

JUNE You should have had a leaflet. Put through.

DAD (*calls*) Mam. Have we had a leaflet?
Mam comes out into the hall.

MAM What about?

JUNE The register. Old people in the Council area.
All this is spoken through the open crack of the door.

MAM (*mouthing to Dad*) I threw it away. (*Pause.*) We're not Council tenants. You've got mistaken.

JUNE Hello?

DAD Yes?

JUNE Rhodes, Arthur. Rhodes, Elizabeth Mary.

DAD Well?

JUNE It's not confined to Council tenants. It's all senior citizens in the Council area. We have you down as pensioners.

MAM (*mouthing*) Ask her for her card.

DAD She looks right enough.

MAM She should have a card. There was a woman at Bramley gagged with her own tights, and they said they were gasmen.
Suddenly the card is held round the door and moved up and down. Dad takes it and hands it to Mam. He then unchains the door. It is a girl in her early twenties, wearing a cape.
Does this reckon to be you? June Potter?

JUNE Yes.

MAM The hair's different.

JUNE I wasn't in Social Services then. I was Transport. I had it frizzed out. They tend to be more relaxed in Social Services.

MAM It's not the same colour.

JUNE I'd just got back from Torquay.

DAD It is her.

JUNE I might have had it dyed, then. I can't remember.

MAM Dyed?

JUNE A cream rinse.

MAM I thought you said you worked for the Council. My uncle
worked for the Council, and you'd never see him without a
collar and tie.

DAD They all dye their hair nowadays. Lads. Everybody.

MAM He wore a suit every day of his life did my uncle.

JUNE Social Services they make us wear what we like.

MAM That's one of them poncho affairs, isn't it?

DAD Well, I've seen Princess Anne in one of them.

MAM Not since she got married.

JUNE It's just a matter of one or two questions.

DAD Fetch her inside. She's only young.

MAM You keep saying that. Youth's no guarantee nowadays.
There was a woman attacked in the Grasmeres and it left her a
vegetable. Wipe your feet.
June comes in and they go through into the living room, as Mam says:
If you want to come waltzing into people's houses you ought to
get yourself a little costume. You'd look heaps better in a
two-piece, and you'd find people much more forthcoming. She
wants to take a leaf out of our Margaret's book.

DAD They can't all be like our Margaret.

MAM That's a change, coming from you. Sit down. Do you want
some tea?
June nods and Mam goes out to the kitchen.
Sending out questionnaires. They want to do something about
public toilets. Stuff written up on walls. Them little rings from
beer cans you see lying about everywhere – never mind
questionnaires.
*Dad has been embarrassed by all this, and is more anxious to put
June at her ease.*

DAD She's hyper-careful, is Mam.

JUNE No, full marks. There are very few people your age
know how to answer the door. I wish I could show her to
Mr Farquarson. At night I walk down the middle of the road.

Pause.

DAD I like those poncho things, personally.

JUNE Mr Farquarson tells us not to dress up. Otherwise we get into an 'us' and 'them' situation. (*Pause.*) These are in fact old ski pants.

Dad nods. Pause.

DAD Not them jogging things?

JUNE No.

Pause.

DAD Not a jogger?

JUNE No fear. (*Pause.*) Thin enough!

June prepares her interviewing kit – clipboard, form, pencil – very methodically.

DAD What's it to do with, this questionnaire?

JUNE No. (*She reads from her notebook as if talking to a child.*) 'Where possible, interviewer should endeavour to see all members of the household together.' I've never done this before, so I have to stick to the book of words. (*Pause.*) You know . . . structured.

DAD Don't want telling two different tales. (*Pause.*) Tip-top job, now, working for the Council.

JUNE They took me on to do discs. Controlled parking.

DAD *and* JUNE (*together*) Transport.

JUNE Then the inevitable happened. Computers. I went and saw Mr Stringfellow and he said, 'My advice to you, June, is to do a bit of a sideways jump and get yourself into the SS.' Social Services.

DAD We don't have a parking problem. We don't have a car.

JUNE I prefer working with people to cars. They're more unpredictable but they're more rewarding. With me people come first. Old people specifically. Older people.

Pause.

DAD They are a problem.

JUNE Yes.

DAD Where to put them. They have to be put somewhere.

Pause.

JUNE Old people?

DAD Cars. I've often thought, if we had one I could put one of those carport affairs inside the front gate. There's room.

JUNE As I see it, young people have a lot to give old people, and old people have a lot to give young people. You know . . . caring.

DAD I agree. With a car our daughter can run us to Ilkley. Or Knaresborough. Will you be motorised?

JUNE I've got my trusty moped, only the clutch has packed in, so I'm sampling public transport.

DAD Your parents'll have a car?

JUNE Split up.

DAD Oh. (*Pause.*) That's on the up and up.

JUNE What?

DAD Divorce.

Mam returns with the tea things.

MAM How do you like your tea? We like ours strong.

JUNE Weak, please. No milk.

MAM No milk?

JUNE No milk.

MAM Whatever for?

DAD Because that's how she likes it.

JUNE I generally have lemon. I don't want lemon but that's what I have.

DAD I've seen our Margaret have lemon.

MAM Only in a café. We haven't got any lemon.

DAD We've got one of those plastic squirters. Lemon juice.

JUNE That'll do.

Dad gets up to go into the kitchen.

MAM And Dad. Some little plates.

He goes.

All that's come in now. Lemon in your tea. Yogurt. Carrying babies on your back. We weren't brought up to any of that. I was thought a bit revolutionary for having prunes.

Dad returns with the plastic lemon and plates.

Not them plates, Dad. The *side* plates. (*She goes out.*)

DAD You're not bothered about side plates? (*calling*) She's not bothered about side plates.

MAM (*calling from the kitchen*) She wants a scone.

JUNE (*to Dad*) I don't want anything to eat.

DAD (*calling*) She doesn't want anything to eat.

MAM (*returning*) You'll have a scone?

JUNE No. I'm on a diet. I get migraine.

MAM From scones?

JUNE It's a special-type non-gluten diet. They've only just
pinpointed it. I haven't to have flour.

DAD It's a terrible scourge, migraine. Our daughter gets
migraine.

MAM Not from scones. It's chocolate with her. I've never heard
of anyone getting headaches from scones.

DAD Look at me. I can't do with tomatoes.

MAM That's your bowels.

DAD (*embarrassed*) Mam.

MAM (*poised with the plastic lemon*) One squirt or two squirts?

DAD Let her squirt it herself.

JUNE One, please.

Mam squirts it.

Now. Can we start? This is the leaflet you should have had and
I will read it to you.

DAD Mam threw it away.

MAM I didn't throw it away. It got thrown away.

JUNE (*reading*) 'In recent months there have been one or two
mishaps involving old people, senior citizens who have become
isolated within the community. Some genuine tragedies have
occurred. Accordingly your Council has decided to compile
a register of all persons of pensionable age within the Council
area. The establishment of such a register will . . .'

MAM Hypothermia.

June stops.

Is that it? Hypothermia? Not us. (*She points.*) We've got a
Dimplex. Background heating.

DAD Plus a fire.

MAM Dimplex and a fire.

DAD For company.

MAM The fire's company. The Dimplex isn't company.

DAD I didn't say the Dimplex was company.

JUNE Anyway. That takes care of question seven: source of
heating. Any heating in the bedroom?

MAM Him.

DAD Mam.

MAM This is old people. It's not us. You want Miss Venables over the road. She has a pacemaker and her friend comes in from Bramley.

June has been told to expect such a reaction, and covertly consults her notebook.

JUNE Hang on . . . 'The refusal to recognise the approach of old age and the possibility of infirmity is entirely natural . . . and in its way commendable.' That was Mr Farquarson, last week. (*She laughs in a stilted way.*) You are as old as you feel. But let me sketch out a possible scenario. You're not feeling too clever; you're in bed. Mr Rhodes goes to fetch the milk, it's slippy and bang, that's his hip gone. Hearing a shout you get up, go downstairs and try shifting him. You promptly have a dizzy do and bang, that's two of you lying on the path in sub-zero temperatures. You won't last long.

Pause.

MAM The point is, we don't want roping in for any get-togethers.

DAD That's it. They put you on a register, next minute you're sitting round banging a tambourine.

JUNE (*reading again*) No. 'When your Council has compiled the register a number of Old People's Wardens will be appointed, whose job it will be to keep track of all old people in the area, particularly those who are "at risk".'

MAM Oh. It's 'at risk' is it? That's something else that's come in, 'at risk'. There never used to be that, did there, 'at risk'. It's all 'at risk' now. Battered babies, battered wives . . . Are you sure you won't have a scone?

JUNE No.

DAD You do read some shocking stories. There was an old lass at Moortown got eaten by her own Alsatian.

MAM Her own silly fault. I wouldn't have an Alsatian. They always revert. We don't want pestering to go to bingo. Joining in. That's what choked us off with church.

JUNE This isn't bingo, Mrs Rhodes. This is survival.

Pause.

DAD We aren't good mixers, that's the trouble.

MAM You're not. I am. I used to be a right good mixer.

DAD You never were.

MAM I went to the Fellowship.

DAD When they lassooed you first. We're neither of us anything in the mixing line. We were when we were first married but you lose the knack.

June makes a note.

MAM What is it you're writing down?

JUNE Nothing.

MAM What did we say?

JUNE Nothing. (*There is a silence. June doodles embarrassed on her pad, then talks while she's doodling.*) Mr Farquarson said that the survey would be a chance for us to do a little ad hoc assessment. Part of our training. You know, fieldwork. Only I'm not supposed to tell you that.

MAM We're guinea pigs.

DAD She has to learn.

MAM Not on us she doesn't.

JUNE I was just noting you both seem very alert mentally.

DAD There you are.

MAM Mentally?

JUNE And you quarrel. That's another good sign.

MAM We never do. We never have a wrong word.

JUNE You don't agree always. You *spar*. Look on it as a sign of life. Vitality. On a scale of one to ten you've got eight.

MAM Why not ten?

JUNE Nobody gets ten. The Queen Mother wouldn't get ten. This is the joy of the job for me. I did surveys in Transport . . . traffic projections, long haul or short haul, purpose of trip . . . only there was no feedback. The beauty of this is . . . it's people. This is what they call interaction.

A long pause with interaction notably absent.

What were we saying?

Mam won't speak.

You were talking about church. How you used to go to church.

DAD They got this new young vicar.

MAM (*reluctantly*) It was the singing we liked.

DAD He kept wanting these discussions. Forums. Race. Religion. Current affairs. We stopped going.

JUNE That's a pity.

MAM Why, do you go to church?

JUNE No.

DAD That's with you being educated. God's always the first
casualty. One time he had us all talking about Buddha. Well,
Mam doesn't know anything about Buddha. And I don't know
anything about Buddha. And the Third World.

MAM I don't even know where that is. We just haven't been
educated.

DAD No dog collar. Always wore civvies. It's as if they're
ashamed of it.

MAM Last time we went to church, in the middle of the
service he suddenly gets up and says, 'Now, I want you all
to shake hands with the person on either side of you.' Well
Dad was all right because he was sat on the aisle, so he'd
only to shake hands with me, but I got a right common
woman in a leopardskin coat. I'd never seen her before in
my life.

JUNE But that's good, isn't it?

MAM Yes, I can see you're in the same brigade.

JUNE Isolation, that's the bugbear.

MAM We don't mind a bit of isolation. It's the other *we* don't
like. He had a couple kissing on the front of the parish
magazine. Christian Love. I'd prefer little kiddies with rice
bowls, I would.

DAD I don't see that God is to do with mixing. Too much God,
and it puts the tin hat on it.

MAM What about you, do you mix?

JUNE I tend to run across people at work. I'm not at risk. I'm not
old.

MAM Old, old. There's risks with youth. You might commit
suicide. That's snowballed.

DAD Mam.

MAM Well. How old are your parents?

DAD Nay, they've split up, haven't they?

MAM Split up? Are you married?

JUNE No.

MAM Where do you live?

JUNE Kirkstall.

MAM They've knocked most of it down. Is it a flat?

JUNE A bedsitter.

MAM A bedsitter? Child of a broken home, living in a bedsitter in one of these inner city areas: you're the one that's at risk. You want to get *yourself* on a register. Coming round telling us. Isolated. We like being isolated. We're like that. It's the same as the radio now, every programme you turn on, it's folk ringing up. And they make out you're all friends. Everybody friends. Well, we're not friends. We've got each other, and that's enough.

JUNE But that's it. You won't always have each other.

MAM Oh, hell and damnation. Do you think we don't know that? Youth.

JUNE I'm not youth. Don't call me youth. I wish I was youth.

DAD (*comfortingly*) You are youth.

Pause.

JUNE Can I have that scone?

MAM Go on.

June eats the scone slowly.

DAD Some more tea?

He gets her it. June has got out an exercise book and is looking through it.

MAM What's that?

June is on the edge of tears.

JUNE My notes. 'Conduct of Interviews' . . . I've gone wrong somewhere . . . It's my fault . . . we're in a confrontation situation now . . . Well, you shouldn't get into a confrontation situation, Mr Farquarson says, you get into a confrontation situation, you've slipped up . . . Cars – it's much more open and shut. It's just a case of, 'Do you mind telling me your ultimate destination. Thank you. Drive on.' I'm maybe not suited to people.

She blows her nose.

DAD You are. I'm sure you are. You're doing champion. We're not good at interviews, probably, are we, Mam?

MAM Have this other scone.

June takes it and eats it quickly.

That's right.

JUNE Transport, I was in a rut. Mr Stringfellow said, 'Take this sideways jump, June, and there'll be so many more doors open to you.'

DAD Listen. You did right. We've got a daughter. *She's* ambitious. 'Life is for living.' That's her motto.

JUNE Well, let's have another go. (*She takes up the clipboard again.*) This is Margaret, is it?

MAM Yes.

JUNE That's question four. (*She reads again.*) 'The Council does not aim to replace family responsibility, only to supplement it, particularly in cases where senior citizens are childless.' So you're not childless. You've got a daughter.
She writes down 'Margaret'. Mam and Dad look at one another.
Any other siblings? I didn't know that either. It means brothers and sisters. No?
Mam looks at Dad again.

DAD (*firmly*) No.

JUNE Is Margaret married?

MAM No. Are you married?

JUNE No.

DAD She could have been married. Married three or four times over if she wanted.

MAM You'll have boyfriends?

JUNE Oh yes. And lives where?

DAD London. Where else?

MAM She has a flat.

DAD She's a personal secretary.

JUNE (*writing*) A secretary.

DAD No, not a secretary. A personal secretary. Her boss is to do with this ceramic heating.

JUNE I've not heard of it.

DAD We hadn't heard of it. It's these heated pottery panels. Set in. And being pottery it retains the heat without running up a lot of expenditure on electricity. I've got a lot of literature about it if you're interested.

MAM She's not interested, Dad. It's only with it being our Margaret that she's interested. Ceramic heating!

DAD She could have gone to university if she'd wanted. But she said, 'Dad, I want to get on with life.' So she took a secretarial course and started off at Brunskill's in Cardigan Road. It was just an ordinary job in the office, with no responsibility. But as Margaret says, 'You make your own responsibility.' It was

old Mr Brunskill picked her out, saw she wasn't like half the
girls in offices, just marking time till they find the right man.
She's never been all that interested in the opposite sex, our
Margaret.

MAM It was always, 'What does he do? Does his work take him to
faraway places?' She had a passion for geography. It was always,
'Get out the atlas, Dad. Show me Perth. Rio de Janeiro.' I said
to her last time she was home, 'Did you ever dream you'd be in
Valparaiso?' But she's very modest, just laughed.

JUNE I'd like to travel. I never go anywhere.

MAM Daughters, they used to live round the corner. All that's
gone.

DAD She comes up to see us whenever her schedule permits. She
flies to Leeds sometimes. Takes air travel in her stride. More
people are killed on the roads. It's a new breed.

JUNE When did she come up last?

DAD When did she come up, Mam? It's only a week or two since.

MAM March.

DAD As long as that? It's with speaking to her on the phone.

JUNE Question three. (*She ticks it off.*) So you're on the phone.

DAD Margaret made us have one installed so she could keep in
touch.

MAM It was for her convenience. She has to have the phone
when she's here anyway. Last time her boss rang up in the
middle of the night wanting her to fly to Düsseldorf.

DAD She says the telephone is one of the tools of her trade. She
won't be much older than you and she's on a five-figure salary.

MAM You won't be badly off, will you, love? The Council, it's a
good job these days. My uncle worked for the Council.

DAD It's not like the private sector.

MAM You've got the satisfaction, though, haven't you? Helping
people.

DAD I noticed you didn't take sugar. Margaret doesn't take sugar.
She has a bit of a struggle with her figure. Has to steer clear of
the carbohydrates. It's all these business lunches. She could
have whatever she wanted to drink but it's generally, 'May I
please have an orange juice.' Left on her own she'd as soon
have a bit of cheese and an apple.

MAM You've got a better figure than our Margaret.

DAD Has she? I'd've thought they were about the same. (*He gets some snaps.*) This is her. Taken at Turin Airport.

MAM She dresses very simply. Crisp white blouse. A few well-chosen accessories.

DAD (*showing her a snap*) Amsterdam. She can look stunning, but her aim is to blend in with the background. She says an ideal secretary should not be noticed, just taken for granted. (*showing her another*) Los Angeles.

MAM Though she can tick people off. She put a woman in her place at Leeds and Bradford Airport. I was embarrassed. I don't know where she gets that from. Not Dad, anyway. He never speaks up. Have you travelled?

JUNE Only Spain.

MAM Everybody seems to have been to Spain now. Except us. They've been to Spain next door. They fetched us a little doll back. It was nothing. We like Scarborough.

DAD Margaret goes all over. You'd be staggered if I told you her itinerary. I've got to know the names of airports just from listening to her converse. Paris: Charles de Gaulle. Chicago: O'Hare. Rome: Fiumicino. Her boss would be lost without her.

MAM But that's all it is, purely professional. He's married with two grown-up sons, one of them at veterinary college. Our Margaret's like a friend of the family. She's spent Christmas with them.

DAD Only because she couldn't get up here.

JUNE And you don't have a car?

DAD No.

MAM We could have done. We could just about have run to a car but Dad wouldn't learn.

DAD It makes it more of a treat when Margaret comes up. Last time she ran us out to Fountains Abbey.

JUNE So 'no car'.

MAM You've got your poise back now, love, haven't you? Asking your questions. It's just a case of having confidence.

JUNE Thank you.

A pause, before Dad reverts to his one topic of interest.

DAD She's got confidence, our Margaret. She's quite at home in hotels. Can choose from a menu without turning a hair. And she knows all the vintage years. But when it comes to her, as I say, it's, 'Can I just have an orange juice, please.'

MAM Where have your parents split up to?

JUNE Mam's in Armley. I don't know where my dad is. I'm always going down home.

MAM That's nice. Nice for your mam.

JUNE Nice for us both. This old people's warden will just keep a quiet eye on you. You won't even know he's there.

MAM It's a him, is it?

JUNE It could be a her, either.

DAD That's the law nowadays, isn't it? Has to be a him or a her. When our Margaret was first starting there was none of that. She had to fight every inch of the way.

MAM Oh, Dad. Not fight.

DAD You don't know. We get postcards from all over. I've got books full. If we had grandchildren it would be a real geography lesson. Where's the one we had from Washington?

MAM Upstairs. In my drawer.

JUNE It doesn't matter.

MAM No, let him.

Dad has gone. June is on her feet ready to go.

Sit down. (*urgently*) Sit down, love.

June sits down.

We've told a lie. We have two children. We had a son. After Margaret. Colin. Only he wasn't right. He's in a home near Otley.

JUNE That's all right. I don't need to know that. Your daughter's the one that matters.

MAM We never talk about it to anybody. We never talk about it to each other. We ought to do, only he won't.

JUNE I won't write it down (*She is nonplussed, not really wanting to know, either, and hides her confusion by consulting her notebook.*)

MAM We thought he was all right, only our Margaret could tell. She wouldn't play with him. Wouldn't have anything to do with him. In the finish we couldn't cope. We waited too long, I think. He was born after Dad got back from the war. We reckon to go once a month only they don't run enough buses. He knows us. We just go and sit out on a seat somewhere, weather permitting. He'd miss us if we didn't go.

146

JUNE   I don't know what to say. It's not to do with this, that. It's more . . . private.

MAM   He's like a child. I look at him and think, well if he was a proper lad he'd be married now, with grown-up kiddies. Margaret won't marry. She's not the marrying sort. She's happy, that's the main thing.

JUNE   I get the impression . . . correct me if I'm wrong: she wouldn't come back, Margaret. I mean, say something happened . . . to look after you.

MAM   I never said that.

JUNE   No. But . . . they tell us to listen to the things you're not saying. Mr Farquarson says that the things you're not saying are more important than the things you are saying.

MAM   What about this other?

JUNE   I don't know.

They sit, June smiling with embarrassment. Dad is coming back.

MAM   Don't say I said.

June shakes her head. Dad comes in with the postcard.

DAD   (*sarcastially*) Your drawer! It was in the scullery. Washington.

JUNE   Nice.

MAM   It'll be all cars, same as everywhere else.

DAD   I've been abroad a bit myself.

MAM   He was in Tunisia.

DAD   Not only Tunisia. Tunisia. Libya, North Africa, Sicily. I saw Monty once. He came past in a jeep and waved. It's not many people can say that.

JUNE   One last thing. In the event of an emergency, say you're both ill, who looks after you?

DAD   Well, we wouldn't both be ill, would we?

JUNE   I'm trying to look ahead.

DAD   We shouldn't want our Margaret coming back, would we? She's got her own life to lead.

MAM   We should just have to manage.

JUNE   Supposing the worst came to the worst. There was just one of you.

DAD   She'd come back. Only I wouldn't let her. I discussed it with her once. She said, 'Well, Dad. We all get older. Life is for living, that's my philosophy.' I don't think you should expect it of your children.

MAM I looked after my mother.

DAD You weren't a career woman.

JUNE No close neighbours? Nobody who could come in?

MAM Next door'd come in all right, given the chance. Don't put her down.

June makes a final note and closes her file.

JUNE The only other thing is to give you this card.

She fishes in her bag for a card, one of a bunch. She gives one to Dad. He looks at it. It says 'HELP!' in large red letters.

It's just in case we have a winter like last year. If for some reason or other you can't get out. You pop this in the window and the warden'll know to call.

DAD (*reading the card*) 'Help!' Bit stark is that, isn't it?

JUNE It says it all, that's the point. You haven't got to be ashamed of asking for help, particularly now you're older. Everybody's getting them, the old, the disabled.

MAM (*drily*) People 'at risk'.

JUNE That's right.

They are in the hall.

DAD It's been a nice change for us talking to you. We don't get many visitors.

JUNE Don't thank me. It's you that's done me the favour. Helped me with my course. Mr Farquarson says, 'Sit and chat. Learn how to draw people out. Get them talking. That's your job.'

June catches Mam's eye and looks away, confused. She has turned them into guinea pigs again. Dad opens the door.

DAD Good luck with your chosen career.

JUNE You too. Well, your retirement anyway.

MAM And think on, try and find yourself a man.

DAD You do what you want.

June lingers, not having mastered the art of leaving.

Happiness, that's the main thing.

JUNE Anyway . . .

And on this tentative note she closes the door. They go back into the living room. Dad sits down in the easy chair. Mam stands by the window. Pause.

DAD She seemed nice enough.

Mam doesn't say anything.

MAM She wants to find herself a chap.

Pause.

DAD What do I do with this card 'Help?' What d'you think?

MAM It's telling the whole street. We'll keep it, just in case. I'll put it in my drawer.

DAD We won't let our Margaret see it. (*Pause.*) Makes you feel older.

Pause.

MAM More leaves coming down. Mess.

Pause.

It never stops.

It is dusk and she begins to draw the curtains. We cut to the outside of the house. The lights are on in the room. We see her finish drawing the curtains and the last chink of light disappears.

Rolling Home

CAST AND CREDITS

MR WYMAN	John Barrett
VAL	Maureen Lipman
MOLLY	Pat Heywood
HAROLD	Bernard Gallagher
DONALD	David Threlfall
VIC	David Foxxe
MATRON	Isabelle Lucas
PAM	Anna Quayle
MR RISCOE	Jack Le White
MR METCALF	Leslie Pitt
ALBERT	Ernest Jennings
ERNEST	Charles Simon
KEVIN	Geoffrey Staines
MISS MUSCHAMP	Gladys Spencer
ALICE	Jeanne Doree
CONNIE	Beatrice Shaw
HANNAH	Molly Veness
NURSE	Michael Worsley
Directed by	Piers Haggard
Designed by	Ray Cusick
Music by	Geoffrey Burgon

EXT. HOSPITAL. DAY.
Various shots: buildings, car park, etc. The odd patient or medical orderly passing. Some visitors arriving.

INT. CORRIDOR. DAY.
A long, institutional corridor in a nineteenth-century building – a workhouse, probably, that has been converted into a hospital. It has been painted cream and some attempt has been made to modernise it in small ways. The lamps are modern and there are pictures on the walls. At the end are double doors.
For some moments nothing should happen, and the corridor remain empty, over it the sounds of an old-fashioned hospital. Somewhere someone is washing up, and there is the faint clatter of pans. The double doors open slowly, and an old man comes through in pyjamas. He comes along the corridor towards the camera. He is in his bare feet. He gets quite close to the camera before the doors open again, more quickly, and Vic, a male nurse in a short white coat comes through.
VIC Mr Riscoe. Mr Riscoe.
  From the tone of voice one should be able to tell this flight and pursuit has happened many times before. The old man takes no notice and carries purposefully on, until the male nurse catches him up, steers him round and they go back down the corridor.
  Where was it this time?
RISCOE Scarborough.
VIC Scarborough! You gone off Whitby then?
RISCOE There's no shagging in Whitby.

INT. CORRIDOR. DAY.
Vic and Riscoe go through the doors and there is a further corridor beyond with more radiators along it, and more pictures. Old men sit on some of the chairs by the radiators. Vic takes Riscoe through to the ward at the end of this corridor, and we stay with another old man, Mr Wyman, who sits with his hands on the radiator looking out of the window. We see through the vast window to the grounds of the hospital.

There is a lawn, neat flower beds and a high wall. Donald, another male nurse, is sitting with one of the old men. Vic passes with Mr Riscoe.

VIC On another Awayday, this one. Scarborough!

Donald smiles, then comes and sits with Mr Wyman, adjusting the sheet of paper in his clipboard as he does so. Donald is about thirty.

DONALD Now then, Joey. What day is it?

WYMAN (*pause*) Is it Wednesday? Wednesday.

DONALD Try Saturday.

WYMAN It's more like Wednesday to me.

DONALD What date?

WYMAN *Saturday.* I'm not so daft.

DONALD *Date.*

WYMAN (*shakes his head*) It's raining. I can see that.

DONALD What's four from seven?

WYMAN You can't take four from seven. Oh no. I'm thinking you mean seven from four. Three.

Donald smiles.

Not so daft. Don't ask me money. I never bothered to learn all that when they had the alteration.

Donald writes something down.

Have I passed?

DONALD What day is it?

WYMAN Wednesday. Well, it's Wednesday to me.

DONALD Do you know where you are?

WYMAN I'm on the ward. There's them rhododendrons. (*Pause.*) I sit here every day and still don't know what's the other side of that wall.

Donald groans. Clearly Mr Wyman has said this umpteen times before. But then on this ward most things have been said umpteen times before.

DONALD You do. (*He gets up.*) I'll tell you one thing, Joey. I wish they were all like you.

He helps Mr Wyman to his feet and they start towards the door.

WYMAN By! My leg does hurt.

Donald looks briefly anxious.

DONALD We'll get you a tablet.

EXT. GROUNDS. DAY.
A car draws up. Molly and Harold get out. They are a comfortable couple in their forties.

INT. WARD. DAY.
Vic looks through a window, checks his watch, and moves off down the ward.

VIC Toilet anybody? Speak now. All got clean bums, have we, ready to face our loved ones? What about Jackie? No. You wouldn't dream of it, would you? Mr Metcalf? You haven't got a little parcel saved up for your niece, have you? Right. Where are they this eager, laughing throng laden with Lucozade?
On cue Molly, Mr Wyman's daughter, comes through the double doors with her husband, Harold.

MOLLY Now then, precious. Have you been waiting?
She gives him a kiss and sits down.

WYMAN What've you come today for?

MOLLY Why? It's Saturday.

WYMAN I thought it was Wednesday.
Molly looks at Harold.

HAROLD (*shrugs*) Well, I'm getting like that now.
He goes and gets a chair from another radiator. They sit in silence looking out of the window.

MOLLY It's next week Stephen's going in for his bronze medal.

WYMAN Which is Stephen?

MOLLY The youngest, Dad. Paul, Melanie, then Stephen. You know Stephen. You were big pals, you and Stephen. I brought you those snaps.

WYMAN What snaps?

MOLLY In a little leather case. We bought it for your birthday. To keep on your locker. You said it was the one thing you'd been wanting. (*aside*) I bet it's been pinched.

HAROLD No.
Pause. She mouths, 'He can't remember Stephen.' She blows her nose.

It's hot is this radiator. The heating side of it's tip-top.

MOLLY We thought Val'd be here. We were expecting to see her.

HAROLD She has to fit it in with her appointments.

MOLLY Well, so do we.

WYMAN I keep looking at yon wall.

HAROLD What wall? (*He looks.*) Why? It's only a wall.

MOLLY Melanie's no different. She's got a little spot on her chin. Taking up all her time. You know what they're like at that age. How's your foot? About the same, is it, your foot?

WYMAN It's about the same.

MOLLY (*aside to Harold*) How long has he had it?

HAROLD What?

MOLLY His foot.

HAROLD I don't know.

Mr Riscoe appears in his pyjamas and makes for the corridor exit. Harold sees him go.

MOLLY Your hands have gone nice, Dad. Haven't his hands gone nice, Harold? Real lady's hands. Never think you were a bricklayer.

HAROLD No. Man of leisure now. Everything done for you.

INT. CORRIDOR. DAY.

Cut to corridor outside. Val, Molly's sister, slightly younger and an altogether smarter woman, is walking along the corridor. Mr Riscoe pads past her. Val looks perplexed. Harold comes through the doors.

HAROLD Hold on, old lad. You're not supposed to go on your travels. Hold on. Hallo, Val.

Donald comes out in pursuit of Mr Riscoe.

DONALD Thanks.

HAROLD He fair shifts, doesn't he?

DONALD Oh ay. Could play for the under twenty-ones, this one.

He takes the old man back in, and Harold and Val follow into the ward.

INT. WARD. DAY.

HAROLD Here's Val.

Val gives a brave smile.

VAL Dad. (*kissing him*) Mol. Have I had a journey! Easterly Road packed solid. Football fanatics. I've been in Bradford all morning.

MOLLY We were just saying how his hands have gone nice. Haven't his hands gone nice, Val?

VAL He looks thinner. You look thinner to me, love. (*She turns away and mouths to Molly.*) I wonder if they get enough to eat.

Molly and Harold exchange looks.
They talk about cutbacks, yet they keep the heating on at this
pitch. I always have a sinus do when I've been here. The air's
that dry. (*Pause.*) Off to Harrogate next week, Dad. My annual
jaunt. Northern Fashion Show.
MOLLY Val's a buyer for a gown shop, Dad.
VAL He knows that. You know that, love, don't you?
MOLLY He forgets.
HAROLD It's to be expected. Look at me. I can never remember
our postcode.
MOLLY DS7 2NU.
HAROLD (weakly) Yes.
VAL I'm RB6 4A. (*Pause.*) Mr Stillman says that if things go
on the way they're going on, there's no reason why next year
I shouldn't eventually have a stab at Paris. Fancy, Dad, your
little Val in Paris.
MOLLY Stephen's going in for his bronze medal.
HAROLD You told him that.
MOLLY I'm telling Val.
HAROLD Are you being affected by the recession? We've been
having a bit of a downturn.
VAL Well, Harold, I think I'm entitled to say 'What recession?'
With our class of customer it really makes no odds. Woman
came in the other day. In the shop ten minutes. Spent six
hundred pounds. I wondered whether I'd be seeing little
Stephen today. Or Melanie. What's happening to all my
nephews and nieces?
MOLLY It's what I was saying: Stephen's doing his bronze
medal and Saturdays is when Paul does his indoor rock-
climbing. Have you come across that, Dad? Indoor rock-
climbing? They do it down the Sports Centre. They have
this make-do rock face, so's when they graduate to the real
thing they don't have to jump in at the deep end. They climb
up on these crampons.
HAROLD Pitons.
MOLLY You haven't been. Rock-climbing, Dad, little Paul. Not
so little now. It was a toss-up between that and hang-gliding.
You've got to let them go their own way.
HAROLD I was just thankful it wasn't pot-holing.

Val is powdering her nose, very bored by Molly's talk of the children.

MOLLY But he's beautifully proportioned is Paul, isn't he, Harold?

HAROLD Well, he's big.

MOLLY Up here now. Bigger than his dad. He said the other day, 'You're getting a bald patch, Dad.' Can look right down on him now.

HAROLD I'll just have a wander out. I'm a bit worried about the car.

VAL What did you have for your dinner, Dad?

WYMAN Oh, one thing and another, you know.

VAL And how's your foot? (*to Molly*) How is his foot?

MOLLY Same. I thought we'd have a word with the nurse before we go. You're not in pain, are you, Dad?

WYMAN No. Only it hurts.

MOLLY Our Melanie, she's got a nasty little spot on her chin. Otherwise we're all champion.
Pause.

EXT. HOSPITAL GROUNDS BY WALL.
Harold is walking round the back of the hospital, inspecting a pile of coke or smokeless fuel. An orderly comes out and puts some rubbish in a large man-size bin.

HAROLD Grand bins.

ORDERLY What?

HAROLD Grand bins. Capacious.

ORDERLY Ay. They have to be.
The orderly goes back inside. Harold wanders on round the hospital.

INT. WARD. DAY.
Donald comes up with a tablet and a glass of water.

DONALD Here we are, Joey.
The old man takes the tablet and swallows it.

MOLLY You see, he takes that like a lamb. At home it would have been a shouting do.

VAL Why do you call him Joey? His name's Wilfred.

DONALD We call them what they like to be called.

VAL Joey makes him sound like a budgie.

MOLLY How is his foot? We wondered if we could have a word.

They follow Donald up the ward to the orderly's room. We pick up Harold as he's walking down the ward, looking for them. He comes into the orderly's room in the middle of the conversation.

INT. ORDERLY ROOM AND CORRIDOR. DAY.

VAL Gangrene? How's he managed to get that?

HAROLD Is this his foot?

DONALD They do at his age. The circulation's poor.

HAROLD That's right.

VAL But he must have got the infection from somewhere. I saw somebody as I was coming in in their bare feet. That's like an open invitation to germs.

MOLLY (*tearful*) Gangrene.

DONALD Sometimes it clears up.

HAROLD Well, if it's not one thing it's another. My mother fell down the cellar steps. It was a two-minute job. I've never been sorry.

DONALD Oh hell. Vic!

Mr Riscoe has gone by again, headed for the door. Donald runs after him.

VAL He doesn't look very sensitive to me. It's a job for most of them, like any other. Funny job for a man anyway, I think, nursing.

MOLLY Why?

VAL Oh . . . odd.

Donald comes back and Mr Riscoe is led away by Vic.

VIC You can't go without your bucket and spade.

MOLLY Why don't you lock the door?

DONALD We can't. Unless they're violent.

HAROLD I think you deserve a medal.

Harold and Val go, Molly turns back.

MOLLY He had a little leather folder. For snaps. We bought it him when he came in, to stand on his locker. He gets confused over his grandchildren.

DONALD It'll be in his drawer. I'll look for it next time.

MOLLY If you would. I know you're busy.

Donald and Molly have been talking outside the office, and we have seen Val kiss Dad and go up the corridor, where she is now waiting to go, Harold with her.

INT. WARD. DAY.

Molly goes back to the ward.

MOLLY We're off now, Dad. Harold's a bit worried about the car so we won't linger. Goodbye, chick. There. I've given you a right good kiss. Ta-ta, pet.

She goes.

INT. CORRIDOR. DAY.

Molly and Harold and Val go through the door and walk down the corridor.

HAROLD It's coke, the central heating. Some sort of smokeless stuff. Beats oil any day.

EXT. GROUNDS AND CAR PARK. DAY.

Molly, Harold and Val leave the hospital and go and stand by Val's car in the car park.

VAL I don't know. You read these stories.

HAROLD What stories?

VAL Old people. Nurses.

MOLLY It's under the Corporation.

VAL We know *that*. I could weep.

MOLLY We couldn't have managed. Up night after night. Paul's got his O Levels to do. I think he's happy.

VAL Gangrene!

HAROLD It's a tip-top place. I mean, this is a cherry tree. And I looked at the menu: they have a choice of puddings.

VAL Mr Stillman asked where my father was. I just said Moortown, but he knew it was a Corporation place, I could tell.

MOLLY We'd no choice. We've been over it again and again. Anyway, I'm not sure he knows where he is.

VAL Well, I do. They have Mr Stillman's mother at home with them. Eighty-odd, and bright as a button. Incidentally, if you want a nice little frock, now's the time. We've got some lovely costumes in, discontinued lines at giveaway prices. They'd suit you.

She kisses Harold and Molly and gets into her car.

HAROLD Belt up.

VAL (*startled*) What?

HAROLD Clunk-click.

VAL Oh.

She goes as Molly and Harold walk over to their car.

HAROLD Don't say it.

MOLLY (*mimicking Val*) Fancy, Dad, your little Val in Paris. Your little Val. She was never his little Val. If she were his little Val why didn't she take him in? She's the single one. Discontinued lines!

He starts the engine and listens.

HAROLD Can you hear a little ticking noise?

MOLLY No.

HAROLD I can. I wouldn't care but it's just been serviced. I reckon they just dust it.

INT. THE WARD. NIGHT.

Vic is going off duty. He and Donald are sat at the night table going through a list of patients, both doing clerical tasks and talking quietly as they do.

DONALD You haven't heard anything?

Vic shakes his head.

VIC She's a real wind-up merchant, that matron.

DONALD It's got to be either you or me.

VIC Neck and neck in the race to get our pips up. I just don't see myself wiping bums ad nauseam.

DONALD It's not that. I need the money.

VIC How is all that?

DONALD Fine.

VIC Named the day?

Donald shakes his head.

It looks like I'm going to be an old maid.

DONALD What happened to the racing driver?

VIC Roared off into the sunset. Usual story. Men just think nurses are a pushover. (*He gets up.*) Anyway, don't do anything I wouldn't do. You do though, don't you?

DONALD It's practically the only time we get.

VIC (*mimicking Matron*) I'm thinking of the patients, nurse.

He goes. Donald is left alone. After a while he walks down the sleeping ward.

INT. CORRIDOR. NIGHT.

A girl is walking down the corridor. She looks through the window into the ward and then goes into the orderly's office.

INT. WARD. NIGHT.

In the ward Donald is checking the beds. He stops and goes to Mr Wyman's locker.

WYMAN Donald.

DONALD You're supposed to be asleep.

He looks in the locker for the folder of photographs, takes it out and puts it on top of the locker.

WYMAN What's that?

DONALD Your family.

WYMAN Buggers.

DONALD Language.

WYMAN You know that wall?

DONALD Why?

WYMAN What's the other side?

Donald is fed up of telling Mr Wyman.

DONALD Oh Joey, it's . . . (*He stops.*) I'll tell you what. I'll go and have a look tomorrow. Then you'll be satisfied. Right? We'll ascertain once and for all. Now go to sleep. Wall!

WYMAN Is it a field?

DONALD Go to sleep.

Donald walks up the ward.

WYMAN It's quiet whatever it is.

Jenny, who is Donald's girlfriend, now comes into the ward. We see them begin to walk slowly up and down the ward between the beds without hearing what they say, until we cut in on the whispered conversation.

JENNY I mentioned savings. He said how much? I said about two thousand pounds.

DONALD Well, nearly. Did he sound pleased?

JENNY Oh yes.

DONALD I think two thousand's good. Did he think it was good?

JENNY Oh yes. He said they were being squeezed by the government. He said that was happening all down the line.

DONALD All what line?

JENNY Just all down the line. Squeezed by the government all down the line.

DONALD But he sounded hopeful?

JENNY Oh yes. Only it's all to do with interest rates.

DONALD Did you tell him I might be going up a grade soon?

JENNY No.

DONALD You should have told him that. It affects our income.

JENNY I said we'd tried the Halifax, and the Bradford and Morley.

DONALD Should you have said that?

JENNY I wondered after. But he laughed. The more the merrier, that's what he said.

DONALD He sounds nice.

JENNY He was nice.

DONALD Did you tell him we'd be willing to become depositors?

JENNY Oh, he said we'd have to become depositors. There wouldn't be any question.

This conversation should be punctuated by the noises of old men sleeping, and with Donald stopping and checking on patients. Pause.
He lives at Lawnswood.

DONALD What's that got to do with it?

JENNY He just happened to say.

DONALD But he sounded hopeful?

JENNY He said they weren't the villains.

DONALD Who?

JENNY The building societies. He said the government was the villain. The economic situation was the villain. He said personally he'd give mortgages on a first-come-first-served basis and none of this to-ing and fro-ing.

DONALD He sounds nice.

JENNY He was nice.

DONALD You should have told him my grading was going up though. Status, that's what they're interested in.

JENNY Have you heard?

DONALD Well, it's between me and Vic.

JENNY He'd have given me some coffee if I'd wanted some.

Donald checks that Mr Wyman is asleep. Donald and Jenny walk back towards the orderly room.

DONALD Did he say when they'd let us know?

JENNY He didn't say.

She breaks down.

DONALD Don't cry.

He kisses her, and they go into the orderly room, out of view. The camera stays in the ward, possibly focuses in on the family pictures in the leather folder, with the sleeping noises and grunting of the old men. Then it slowly goes up the ward past the open door of the orderly room where Donald is embracing Jenny, his white coat still on, trousers round his ankles, bare bum to the camera; but the sound is not the sounds of sex but still of old men sleeping.

INT. CORRIDOR. DAY.

A slow procession of old men. Some have got walking frames, another is being wheeled. Mr Wyman is in a wheelchair, but one foot is now in a slipper. Donald is pushing him. They are all going in the same direction. As the procession moves along, Vic gives a Peter O'Sullivan-type commentary, as he also pushes one of the patients along in a wheelchair.

VIC Come on, lads. Only another four furlongs to go and it's Mr Dyson in the lead. Mr Dyson in the lead with Mr Riscoe coming up on the far side. Mr Riscoe's coming up on the far side but Mr Wyman's making a last-minute bid . . .

Donald is pushing Mr Wyman.

. . . a surprise spurt here by Donald on Mr Wyman, and at the post it's Mr Wyman with Mr Riscoe second and Mr Dyson third.

Donald is laughing, as are some of the old men. It should be a cheerful scene.

INT. ANOTHER CORRIDOR. DAY.

Old women also on the move, also encumbered by walking frames, etc., and surveyed magisterially by Matron, who is black, assisted by three female nurses.

MISS MUSCHAMP I was a big hiker. All during the war. My friend and me. We were in the Bradford Ladies. Went all over. Distance no object.

MATRON Help each other. Keep up, Muriel. Help her, Nora. Imagine we're striding over the moors. Deep breaths. You don't want to keep your boyfriends waiting, do you?

INT. VARIOUS CORRIDORS ETC. DAY.
*The race. Montage of old people walking, music over. Close shots of
feet, walking frames, wheelchairs etc. The two streams finally mingle.*

INT. HOSPITAL. ASSEMBLY HALL. DAY.
*The old men and women have assembled in a hall which also functions
as a theatre. There is a piano. Posters on the walls, notices. Mr Wyman
is at the back. Pam, a jolly therapist in her thirties, is taking the class.*
PAM   Now, is everybody ready? No. We are not ready. Are we,
    Alice? Are we, Ernest? What did I say last week?
    Miss Muschamp puts her hand up.
    Don't tell me, Miss Muschamp, do it. *Mix.* We don't just stay
    in our own little group. Alice, you come over here. Hannah,
    you here. Ernest. We aren't frightened of them, are we, girls?
    They're only men. Some ladies would fall over themselves to
    get a boyfriend like this. That's right, Iris. That's better. No,
    not you, Mr Riscoe. You keep here.
    *Donald half-sits in the window sill, watching. Mr Wyman looks out
    of the window. It is another view of the wall.*
    We'll kick off with a song: 'I've Got Sixpence.'
    *She sits down at the piano and they begin to play. Pam half-turns
    round while she's playing so she can mouth the words at them.
    Mr Wyman isn't singing, but staring out at the wall.*
PAM *and* OLD PEOPLE (*singing*)
    I've got sixpence,
    Jolly, jolly sixpence.
    I've got sixpence, to last me all my life.
    I've got twopence to spend,
    And twopence to lend
    And twopence to send home to my wife.
    No cares have I to grieve me,
    No pretty little girls to deceive me,
    I'm happy as a king, believe me,
    As I go rolling home.
    Rolling home. Rolling home.
    By the light of the silvery moon, *etc.*

EXT. PARK. DAY.

Shot of the outside of the hospital wing, taken from the wall that Mr Wyman is looking at. Faintly, the sound of singing. Singing stops and we go back inside again.

INT. HALL. AS BEFORE.

PAM So it's Gentlemen versus the Ladies, and we're starting off with the names of birds. Names of birds, everybody, please, and Donald's going to keep the score. Off we go.

At intervals throughout the following dialogue an old lady in a wheelchair says, 'I'm not here. I'm not here.' As if to confirm this, no one takes any notice of her.

VARIOUS VOICES Sparrow.

PAM Sparrow.

VOICE Thrush.

PAM Thrush.

VOICE Blackbird.

ANOTHER VOICE Wren.

RISCOE Shitehawk.

VOICE Crow.

PAM Crow, good, yes.

RISCOE Shitehawk.

Vic signals to Pam that Mr Riscoe has a contribution to make.

VIC Pam.

Pam, who has been trying to ignore Mr Riscoe, gives Vic a dirty look.

RISCOE Shitehawk.

PAM I didn't hear that, Mr Riscoe.

VIC Shitehawk.

PAM I'll kill you, Vic.

RISCOE Shitehawk's a bird. They had them in India.

PAM Well, that wouldn't be their real name. Hawk perhaps, but not the other bit.

RISCOE When you came out of the cookhouse with your plate they'd swoop down and pinch your dinner.

PAM I don't believe that, but anyway shall we give it him, ladies? Just this once, seeing he's a man. Come on then, more birds.

Miss Muschamp, who is sitting near Donald and is rather refined, suddenly comes to life.

MISS MUSCHAMP Osprey. Osprey.

DONALD What?

MISS MUSCHAMP Osprey.

DONALD (*calling out*) Osprey here.

PAM Osprey? That's good. Who's that? Miss Muschamp. I might
have known.

MISS MUSCHAMP Kingfisher.

PAM Kingfisher! What colour's that, Connie?
Connie shakes her head.
Blue.

MISS MUSCHAMP Heron. Jackdaw. Magpie.

PAM Heron, yes. Jackdaw, Magpie. Give the others a chance,
Miss Muschamp. They haven't had your education.

VOICE Hen. Hen.

PAM Hen. That's good.

RISCOE Cock.

PAM (*wearily*) Yes, all right, Mr Riscoe.

RISCOE Cock.

PAM I said all right.
Miss Muschamp covers her face.

RISCOE Tits. Tits.
Pam makes a face at Donald.

PAM You spoil it for everybody else, Mr Riscoe. I think we'd
better play Rivers and Seas.
*Mr Wyman is still looking out of the window. Donald follows his
look. It is just the wall.*

INT. TREATMENT ROOM. DAY.
*Donald is bandaging Mr Wyman's foot, which is plainly getting worse.
We see the wall outside. An occasional orderly passes.*

DONALD I've said. I'll go. When I've done this. So shut up about
it. You get on my nerves. It's wall, wall, wall.

WYMAN Don't you tell me. I was a bricklayer. You didn't know
that, did you?

DONALD Yes.

WYMAN I built . . . now then. I built somewhere famous in
Leeds. I built the Queen's Hotel.

DONALD Not single-handed?

WYMAN That hurts.

DONALD Sorry.

WYMAN The Princess Royal opened that. She shook hands with me. Right performance. Hands clean first. Fingernails inspected. Told what to say if she asked me this that and the other. All over in a minute or two. Tap tap. Silver trowel. Did it properly after she'd gone. She'd have never made a bricklayer. Launch ships. Plant trees. Lay bricks. It's a right job.

DONALD What?

WYMAN Royalty.

DONALD Never do this job, though, do they?

WYMAN It hurts like billy-o does that.

DONALD Right, I'll go look on the other side of the wall for you?

WYMAN That's right.

DONALD There's other patients on this ward you know, besides you.

WYMAN You're my pal.

Donald goes out. Mr Wyman stares out of the window and in a moment Donald passes. He pretends to shake his fist at Mr Wyman. Mr Wyman laughs.

EXT. GROUNDS BY WALL. DAY.

When he is safely out of sight of Mr Wyman, Donald waits until it will seem he has had time to go and look beyond the wall. He takes out a cigarette. To the casual onlooker he seems to be skiving. Cut to exterior of the ward block, looking in on the corridor. Matron is passing through and glances out of the window and sees Donald. She stops. She taps on the window. Donald turns. She beckons sternly.

INT. CORRIDOR WITH SEATING AREA. DAY.

Donald comes through looking pissed off. He strides down the ward, going past Mr Wyman without looking at him.

DONALD Now have you all been to the toilet? (*He goes down the corridor, stopping in front of each one.*) Toilet? Toilet? Toilet?

An old man nods.

Come on, then.

OLD MAN No, I've been.

DONALD When?

OLD MAN Just this minute.

Donald feels his trousers.

DONALD Oh, bloody hell.

WYMAN Well, I don't do that. I never do that. I know when
I want to go. I always sing out.

Donald takes no notice and helps the other old man out.

VIC Oh dear. What's got into your friend, then? She's cross.

INT. WARD. NIGHT.

Donald is sat at the night table.

WYMAN Donald.

*Donald takes no notice, at first, then he gets up and goes down the
ward. He stands at the foot of Mr Wyman's bed, but we don't hear
the conversation. He goes and gets a cradle, which he puts under the
bedclothes to lift the clothes off Mr Wyman's feet.*

DONALD Better?

WYMAN Yes.

DONALD I got into bother with you, you know. I was told off.
Flaming wall.

WYMAN I'm sorry.

DONALD Never mind. Night-night.

WYMAN Donald. You never told me. What's there?

*At this point Jenny, Donald's girl, comes and stands waiting for him
just inside the doors of the ward. Donald sees her, so this following
speech is partly done watching her. He sits down by the bed.*

DONALD It's a house. A really nice little house. Two up, two
down. Porch, path up to the door. Honeysuckle. There's a little
garden. Flowers. Apple tree. And a vegetable patch. It's ideal.

WYMAN Who's it belong to?

DONALD A young couple. I think they've just got married.

WYMAN Yes? What's he got in the garden?

Donald hesitates.

DONALD Beans?

WYMAN It could be beans. Beans'd do well. Runner beans.

DONALD Runner beans. Go to sleep. Is that better with your
foot?

WYMAN Runner beans.

*He smiles and closes his eyes as Donald goes back up the ward
where Jenny has opened the door and is waiting for him. He puts his
arm round her and they go out.*

INT. WARD. DAY.

The ward. Mr Wyman sits by his bed in a dressing gown, walking frame by the bed, foot bandaged. Molly and Harold are sitting by the bed, Val also. Pause.

MOLLY Stephen got his bronze medal.

Val gets up, and goes and stares out of the window.

Life-saving. Nice to have something like that up your sleeve. In an emergency.

The leather folder is laid flat on the locker. Molly stands it up.

Our Melanie's got going on this indoor rock-climbing now. Her and Paul. You know, little Paul that's big now? And she's doing another course besides in this Jappy wrestling. They do it at the new centre. I said to her, 'You might as well: there's all sorts of fellers about.' She can throw her dad. You can do anything you want, at the centre, in the way of sports. Harold's even been talking about squash.

HAROLD I'm too old for squash.

MOLLY Nobody's too old for anything these days, are they, Dad? Look at President and Mrs Reagan. We think they've got a look of Mr and Mrs Brewster.

VAL (*returning*) Who?

MOLLY President and Mrs Reagan.

VAL (*sniffs her sleeves*) It gets into your clothes. I go home and I need a complete change of outfit.

Donald passes with an old man.

HAROLD You deserve a medal.

VAL They're nicely off now, nurses. I've no sympathy for anybody that works for the local authority, choose what they do. They aren't living in the real world.

Donald passes with the same old man, walking him back.

They don't lie awake worrying about profit margins, being undercut. I see it in Mr Stillman's face. He went over to Blackpool the other week. A round table on man-made fibres. He was practically the only Englishman there. All Japanese.

MOLLY We're thinking of going in for one of these new fridge-freezers, Dad, did we tell you?

VAL He had some Japanese food. Said it was all right, only more what we'd call hors d'oeuvres really. He had to let three people go last week. All men.

MOLLY Oh dear.

VAL I'm all right. Mr Stillman said to me, he said, 'Don't you worry, Val. The right man for the job is often a woman.'

Donald comes back and Molly gets up.

MOLLY How is his foot?

DONALD About the same.

Mr Wyman raises his hand.

WYMAN Now then, Donald.

VAL He speaks to you. Doesn't speak to us, do you, Dad? We're your family. We love you, chick.

DONALD He's tired.

MOLLY We'll go.

She and Val kiss him. Harold to Donald:

HAROLD You're doing a great job.

They pass Vic, who has just recaptured Mr Riscoe for the seventeenth time that day.

Keep up the good work.

EXT. CAR PARK AND GROUNDS. DAY.

VAL I'm not wasting any sympathy on him. I remember the way he made mother suffer. He killed mother.

MOLLY No . . . It was Gilbert dying that killed mother.

VAL I went in one morning and she was crying and you could see there was a right blotch on her cheek. I said, 'What's that mark, Mam?' She said, 'Oh, nothing I must have been bitten.' He'd hit her.

HAROLD Nobody's perfect.

VAL If something does happen to him we shall have to think what to do about Rothwell Street.

HAROLD Put it on the market.

VAL What market? It's due for demolition all round there. I'm surprised it hasn't been squat. It's all students.

HAROLD They have to live somewhere.

MOLLY Our Melanie fetched a lad in the other night. Mascara.

VAL A lad?

MOLLY He was quite nicely spoken but it was definitely mascara.

HAROLD She'd met him at rock-climbing.

MOLLY Rock-climbing, mascara; you can't add it up, can you?

Val and Molly kiss.

173

VAL I'll be glad when this job's over.

MOLLY Don't say that.

VAL Well, you don't have a job, Mol. I'm a professional woman. I've got other things to think about. I'm in Chesterfield tomorrow.

She gets into her car as they go back to theirs.

MOLLY *Yes?*

HAROLD Nothing.

INT. WARD OR CORRIDOR. DAY.

Mr Wyman sits in a wheelchair at the window, staring out at the wall.

WYMAN Donald.

DONALD What?

WYMAN How are his beans?

DONALD Coming on.

WYMAN Frost. That's the bugbear.

INT. ASSEMBLY HALL. DAY.

Pam and a mixed group of old men and women, as before.

VARIOUS VOICES Cricket.

PAM Cricket, yes.

VOICE Tennis.

PAM Tennis, yes.

VOICE Table tennis, yes.

PAM Table tennis, very good, Connie.

RISCOE Snogging.

PAM Ignoring you, Mr Riscoe.

VOICE Badminton.

PAM Badminton, yes.

RISCOE Shagging.

MISS MUSCHAMP Bridge.

PAM Bridge did you say, Miss Muschamp?

MISS MUSCHAMP Bridge. Chess.

PAM Chess, yes.

MISS MUSCHAMP Croquet. Bezique.

VOICE We can't win if she plays.

PAM Well, you've got to think, Clifford. Compete. That's the name of the game. What about football? Nobody's mentioned football.

ALICE Football.

PAM Good, Alice. Football.

CONNIE Blow football.

PAM Blow football. Very good, Connie.

RISCOE Love.

Pam ignores this.

VIC Mr Riscoe says love.

PAM Love isn't a game, Mr Riscoe. We can't give him love, can we, girls? (*to Vic*) I think you encourage him.

Mr Wyman is sitting as usual by the window, but for once he isn't looking out of it. Cut to outside the room, as Pam starts them up on a song: 'Bye, Bye, Blackbird'. Outside a labourer comes by with a wheelbarrow. Bricks. The sound of singing from inside.

EXT. WALL.

INT. ASSEMBLY HALL. DAY.

Back in the recreation room Mr Wyman has seen the labourer with the wheelbarrow and the bricks. He gets himself to his feet and tries to see out of the window down the wall.

WYMAN They're doing something to the wall.

His neighbours take no notice as they sing and follow Pam in the actions to 'Bye, Bye, Blackbird'. Mr Wyman stands up and addresses the room:

They're doing something to the wall!

Only Donald takes any notice.

INT. CORRIDOR. DAY.

Cut to the old men trailing back along the corridor. Donald wheels Mr Wyman.

DONALD Yes, I'll find out. Stop nattering about it.

Vic is pushing someone in a wheelchair and singing 'You Made Me Love You', waltzing him from side to side in the chair. Matron comes along, overtakes Donald and walks behind Vic.

MATRON Nurse. You won't get your grading that way, nurse.

Vic stops. Matron gives him a black look and goes on. Donald catches up with Vic.

VIC (*ruefully*) Go to Gaol. Go directly to Gaol. Do not pass Go. Do not collect two hundred pounds.

The procession continues.

INT. TREATMENT ROOM. DAY.

*At the wall outside we see bricklayers at work. Mr Wyman is having his
foot treated by Donald. So that when Donald talks about the decay of
the wall he is actually dealing with the decay of the foot.*

WYMAN What sort of repairs? What for?

DONALD Re-pointing. The stone's been eaten away. The mortar's
crumbling. It's sagging in parts. Like me.

WYMAN If it's sagging they'll have to take it down.

Donald says nothing.

I'll maybe see the little house.

Donald says nothing.

Donald.

DONALD What?

WYMAN I'll maybe see the little house.

DONALD How does that feel, Joey?

WYMAN Champion. Champion.

INT. WARD. DAY.

Val, Molly and Harold are talking to Donald.

VAL Can you give us some sort of timetable? It's only so we can
plan ahead. There's a possibility I may have to go to Milan.

MOLLY And Paul's got his O Levels coming up.

HAROLD Yes, only that doesn't matter.

MOLLY Well, we don't want him upsetting.

DONALD He's been a bit better these last few days. His foot's
improved. It seems to have stopped spreading.

VAL I'd prefer to see a doctor. I don't think I ever have seen
a doctor, in all the time we've been coming here.

DONALD He comes round in a morning. He won't be able to tell
you any different.

*They go and Donald goes back into the ward. Mr Wyman is sat
looking out of the window.*

WYMAN Getting nearer.

EXT. DAY.

Men at work, shot through foreground window.

INT. WARD.

Donald and his girl, sat at the night table.

JENNY There's one big room and one little room that would do
as a bedroom. Then there's the kitchen.

She draws him a plan.

DONALD Three rooms. Where's the bathroom?

JENNY The bath's in the kitchen. Under the draining board. It
like lifts up.

DONALD Where's the lav?

JENNY Across the landing. She seems a nice enough woman. She
said she appreciated the plight of young married couples and
was prepared to make an exception for us on that basis.

DONALD We're not married.

JENNY We will be.

DONALD What's she? Widow?

JENNY Divorced.

DONALD She say anything about children?

JENNY I didn't ask her.

DONALD Why?

JENNY I didn't dare.

Donald makes a gesture of despair.

You don't know what it's like. Rushing to be first with the
paper. Trailing round day after day. Ringing up and it being
engaged. I've had it all to do.

DONALD We swore we wouldn't rent.

JENNY We can't buy. What else can we do?

DONALD I don't know.

JENNY Come into the office.

DONALD No. It'll just eat away everything we've got saved up.
Even if it's me gets the grading it'll eat it all away.

INT. WARD. DAY.

*Mr Wyman is in bed. Molly sits on the bed. Harold plays with a
walking frame.*

MOLLY A bit better again today. He looks better. You look better,
Dad. How's your Lucozade? (*She opens his locker.*) Still got
quite a bit in hand. (*She takes out the leather folder of snaps.*)
This belongs on top of your locker, Dad. We want to be where
you can see us, love. (*She puts it on the locker. Pause.*) Our

Melanie's discovered boys. (*Pause.*) I suppose it was only a
matter of time. (*Pause.*) And Paul's limbering up for his
O Levels. (*Pause.*) Stephen's got a verruca. No more life-
saving. Confined to dry land for the time being. They'll just
have to drown. Harold, stop playing about with that thing and
come sit down.
Donald goes by.
Bit better again today.

DONALD That's right.

*Val comes in, limping, her shoe in her hand. Mr Wyman has his eyes
closed.*

VAL I've just gone over on my heel. That path's a quagmire. Forty
quid.

HAROLD You want a drop of that superglue.

MOLLY Bit better again today.

VAL Is he?

MOLLY Asleep.

VAL Better; no better. It's just a prolongation. I'd just like to hear
an authoritative statement from somebody. That nurse knows
nothing, you can tell.

WYMAN (*opening his eyes*) Are you the married one?

MOLLY No. I'm the married one, Dad. That's Val.

VAL He knows perfectly well.

MOLLY He doesn't. He gets confused.

VAL I thought you said he was better.

MOLLY Try and have a bit of understanding. Val's in ladies'
gowns, Dad. She's the career girl.

VAL What's that supposed to mean, career girl?

Harold is still playing with the walking frame.

HAROLD The man that invented these deserves a medal. Light
as a feather. I'm looking forward to having one of these, Dad. I
can't wait.

VAL I only did what Mam wanted me to do. She wanted me to
get on.

MOLLY Yes, but she thought you'd look after them when the time
came. Instead of that, I was the one.

VAL I did my share. I'd have been in London now if it hadn't
been for him.

MOLLY I bore the brunt. And I've got a family of my own.

VAL I've sacrificed. I've sacrificed all down the line. I could have been married. I could have been in London. I could have been a buyer for C&A.

MOLLY Married? You've no need to get married.

VAL What does that mean?

MOLLY Little trips to Manchester. Blackpool. Mr Stillman this. Mr Stillman that. What does Mrs Stillman think?

HAROLD Nay, Mol.

VAL She doesn't think anything, because I'm a friend of the family. She tells me all sorts. They've got a son at York University. The idea. I helped her choose some curtains.

WYMAN Shut up, fratching.

VAL Little trips! It's work.

WYMAN Stop it. The pair of you. (*Pause.*) I loved your mother.

VAL You'd a funny way of showing it.

HAROLD No. No. Shut up. Shut up.

MOLLY Valery Wyman, what a thing to say to your own father.

VAL Hitting her.

MOLLY He never hit her.

WYMAN I hit her once.

VAL You hit her more than once.

HAROLD No. Please. Stop it.

VAL On her breast. That's where you hit her. That's what started it all.

MOLLY Nay, it never is. Doctor Roberts said that was all rubbish.

VAL Mam didn't think so.

Mr Wyman is crying.

MOLLY You've made him cry.

VAL He wants to cry.

HAROLD No.

VAL He should have cried years ago. Me and Mr Stillman. I put in eighteen hours a day at the Northern Fabrics Fair. And you want to ask Mrs Stillman who helped get rid of her sinus. You always had a small mind, Maureen Wyman.

Val stalks out, her exit somewhat spoiled by the fact she is still only wearing one shoe.

HAROLD Dear oh dear.

MOLLY I might as well not be married. You wet hen. You're supposed to stick up for me. That's what marriage means.

INT. WARD. NIGHT.

Donald is sitting by Mr Wyman's bed, holding his hand. Jenny comes in and tiptoes down the ward and stands at the end of the bed. Donald smiles.

DONALD I won't be a sec.

    She smiles. Walks back up the ward towards the orderly's room.

WYMAN Have they got kiddies, that couple?

DONALD What couple?

WYMAN Over the wall.

DONALD Not yet. I shouldn't be surprised if they do, though. Little house, garden. Just right for kiddies. They've got a dog.

WYMAN Dogs are all right. Do you know them?

    Donald hesitates.

    Will you tell them something?

DONALD What?

WYMAN They mustn't have children.

DONALD Why not?

WYMAN No children.

DONALD Don't be so daft, Joey. What sort of a thing is that to say to anybody? Don't have children. They're young. They're just at the beginning. They've got all their lives.

    Wyman has hold of Donald's arm.

    Let go.

WYMAN Tell them. No children.

DONALD I won't. You silly daft sod.

WYMAN Donald.

DONALD Lay off.

    Mr Wyman releases his grip on Donald's arm and slumps back on the pillow. Donald tucks him in.

    Oh Christ. What have you done?

WYMAN I'm sorry.

DONALD Don't say you're starting on this game now. You were supposed to be different. You've spoiled your record, you.

    He goes up the ward.

INT. ORDERLY ROOM. NIGHT.

Donald goes into the orderly's room. Jenny is sitting there. He shakes his head, but doesn't say anything, and gets a sheet out of the cupboard. Camera stays with her.

INT. WARD. NIGHT.
When we go back to the bed the sheets have been changed.
DONALD All right?
> *Wyman nods. Donald checks one or two other patients then goes up the ward towards the lighted doorway of the orderly room. Donald goes in. Cut back to the bed where Wyman is still awake. Eyes open. Camera goes slowly up the ward, pausing at the door of the orderly room, now half closed.*

INT. ORDERLY ROOM. NIGHT.
Donald is kissing Jenny. He breaks off suddenly and listens. She watches him, listening, and listens too. Then he looks down and we hear his trouser zip.

EXT. HOSPITAL GROUNDS. LATE DUSK.
A shot of the lighted windows of the corridor. The door leading out of the corridor into the grounds is open. We see Matron coming down the corridor. She stops at the open door, comes out and looks round. Finding nothing, she goes back inside, closing the door.

INT. CORRIDOR. NIGHT.
Matron comes down the corridor. There is a line of light from the orderly room, which she passes. going straight into the ward.

INT. WARD. NIGHT.
There is no one at the night table at the end of the ward. She walks round the beds. Wyman's bed is empty.

INT. ORDERLY ROOM. NIGHT.
Donald is making love to Jenny on the floor of the orderly room. The door is pushed open, but is stopped by Donald's leg. He looks over his shoulder up at Matron standing in the doorway.
MATRON When you've finished that, nurse, you might just glance in the ward. One of your patients seems to have gone for a walk.

EXT. GROUNDS BY WALL AND CANAL. DAY.
A high-angle shot of an ambulance drawn up on the drive, in front of where the wall is being rebuilt. Two attendants are stepping through the gap with a stretcher on which is a sheeted figure. Beyond, by the

bank of a canal, is Donald, and a couple of policemen and a man in a wetsuit.

EXT. GROUNDS BY WALL AND CANAL. DAY.
Reverse shot of Vic watching from a first-floor window.

INT. CORRIDOR OUTSIDE MATRON'S OFFICE.
Matron is just showing Molly and Harold and Val out.

MATRON Yes. Of course, they do wander at that age. And as I say, we can't lock the doors. Not unless they're violent.

VAL He was never violent. He was much more sweet-natured.

MOLLY The tragedy is he just seemed to be picking up. His foot was better, he . . . anyway.

MATRON Yes. Though, it's all downhill one way or another. At this age.

HAROLD Quite. My mother fell down the cellar steps. All over in two minutes. I think that's the best way.
The camera draws back and we see them shake hands with the Matron. Then they come towards the camera on their way along yet another corridor out of the hospital.

VAL Nice woman. Get them in a uniform and they have a lot of dignity. Very professional, but caring. Whereas we've never even had an apology from that male nurse. What was he doing?

MOLLY They're short-handed.

HAROLD I couldn't blame him. They deserve a medal. I hope he'll not be sacked.

VAL Why? Only he won't be. Nobody's sacked. Not in this day and age.

EXT. GROUNDS BY WALL AND CANAL. DAY.
They are outside, passing the hole in the wall. A bricklayer is at work patching up the hole.

MOLLY I don't know what all that was about, him wanting to know what was the other side.

VAL He knew what was the other side. I've told him a time or two. Just staring and staring and not talking. I got fed up of it. I said, 'I don't know what there's to stare at. There's a wall. And a canal, and beyond it's the cemetery.'

MOLLY He'd be confused, bless him.

VAL They ought to cater for that.
They are walking out of earshot towards the car park.
A hole there. Its a standing invitation. Somebody wants
reporting. But they won't be. You bet.
HAROLD They can't think of everything.

EXT. CAR PARK. DAY.
They are standing by Val's car.
MOLLY He's at peace now, anyway. (*She blows her nose.*)
VAL I mustn't linger. I'm due in Bradford at three to look at
some slipovers. It never stops.
MOLLY Paul's taking part in a demonstration tonight. So we've
got to be on parade. 'Rescue and Resuscitation in Sub-Zero
Temperatures.' He gets wrapped up in tinfoil, apparently.
VAL Ring, anyway. We can liaise about the funeral after the
inquest. Mr Stillman knows someone in the Lions who's an
undertaker and we can both chip in over the eats. (*She leans out
of the car.*) I've got an answerphone now, so you can give me a
tinkle any time and put it on tape. You speak after the tone.
*She drives off. They walk to their car, get in and sit for a moment,
before Harold starts the engine.*
MOLLY Tell me something.
HAROLD What?
MOLLY Why is it we always see her to her car and not the other
way round?
Harold shakes his head.
HAROLD We shan't be doing now, anyway, shall we? We shan't be
coming again.
MOLLY That's not the point I'm making.
*He starts the engine. Another car has meanwhile arrived and a
woman and her husband get out with an old man. As Molly and
Harold drive off, the new trio are going up the steps of the hospital,
as Matron comes out. And we hear her say:*
MATRON Do you know, you're our first Kevin. We've never had a
Kevin before.

INT. WARD. DAY.
*Donald is busy with the new old man. An Asian doctor is on his
rounds, followed by Matron and Vic, who now sports the tabs of his*

higher grading. He also carries a clipboard. The party stops at the new
arrival's bed.

VIC Could you see to this, nurse?

Vic walks away down the ward as Donald draws the curtains round
the bed for doctor's examination of the new admission. It is plain
that Donald has not been upgraded. The doctor and Matron wait as
Donald pulls back the sheet from the old man for the examination.
Overhead shot of the old man lying flat on his back, naked. Music.

Intensive Care

CAST AND CREDITS

FATHER	Frank Crompton
MIDGLEY	Alan Bennett
JOYCE MIDGLEY	Helen Fraser
AUNTY KITTY	Thora Hird
UNCLE ERNEST	Colin Douglas
HARTLEY	Derek Fowlds
JEAN	Madge Hindle
MARK	Jeremy Mosby
ELIZABETH	Karen Tunstall
VALERY	Julie Walters
ALICE DUCKWORTH	Elizabeth Spriggs
COLIN MIDGLEY	David Major
MRS MIDGLEY'S MOTHER	Jeanne Doree
MISS TUNSTALL	Joan Sanderson
TEACHER	Ted Beyer
MRS AZAKWALE	Lucita Lijertwood
MR HORSFALL	Jim Broadbent
HEADMASTER	Aubrey Morris
DENIS'S MOTHER	Alison Lloyd
DENIS'S FATHER (YOUNG)	Anthony Addams
DENIS AS A BOY	Kirk Wild
HEATHER	Karen Petrie
1ST NURSE	Pamela Quinn
2ND NURSE	Trish Roberts
INDIAN DOCTOR	Shope Shodeinde
FAT MAN	Frank Birch
YOUNG MAN ON TELEPHONE	Alan Hulse
ORDERLY/PORTER	Johnny Leeze
WOMAN ON STICKS	Frances Cox
DAY MATRON	Brenda Hall
WOMAN ON TELEPHONE	Olive Pendleton
VERY YOUNG DOCTOR	Peter Chelsom
HOSPITAL CLERK	Alan Starkey
Directed by	Gavin Millar
Designed by	Humphrey Jaeger
Music by	Jim Parker

INT. HOSPITAL CORRIDOR. DAY.

A long, featureless corridor in a modern hospital. Empty. Double doors at the end. The camera tracks slowly along the corridor towards the double doors. Suddenly, the doors swing open and a trolley with an elderly man on it is pushed madly along the corridor by a resuscitation team, the camera retreating very rapidly before it until more double doors close off the scene.

INT. MIDGLEY'S HOME. KITCHEN. DAY.

Midgley, a man of thirty-nine, sits at a kitchen table looking into the camera. He has his overcoat on. A carving knife is in front of him on the table.

MIDGLEY I just never expected it.

VOICE OVER (MISS TUNSTALL) On the many occasions Midgley had killed his father, death always came easily. He died promptly, painlessly and without a struggle. Looking back, Midgley could see that even in these imagined deaths he had failed his father. It was not like him to die like that. Nor did he.

MIDGLEY The timing is good. It's only my father who would stage his farewell in the middle of a Meet the Parents week.

Mrs Midgley seizes the carving knife and slices the crust viciously from Midgley's sandwiches. She looks disgusted.

INT. MIDGLEY'S SCHOOL. DAY.

Midgley and another teacher come through double doors, thread their way through a crowd of parents and children and go into the school hall.

MIDGLEY I notice how young the parents are getting. Fathers in particular. They even have permed hair, the odd earring . . . features I still find it hard to forgive in the children.

Miss Tunstall, the school secretary, hands them several folders.

OTHER TEACHER I saw one with a swastika necklace.

MIDGLEY A boy?

OTHER TEACHER A parent.

MIDGLEY There's a mother somewhere with green hair.

MISS TUNSTALL Not just green. *Bright* green. And then you wonder the girls get pregnant.

Miss Tunstall goes to the door of the hall and addresses the waiting crowd.

MISS TUNSTALL Thank you.

Parents and children flood into the hall seeking out teachers. Cut to Midgley being interviewed by Mrs Azakwale, a large black lady.

MRS AZAKWALE Coretta's bin havin' these massive monthlies, Mr Midgley. Believe me en twenty years I en never seen menstruatin' like it.

MIDGLEY It's her poor performance in Use of English that worries me.

MRS AZAKWALE She bin wadin' about in blood to her ankles, Mr Midgley. I en never out of the launderette.

Behind Mrs Azakwale, waiting his turn, is Mr Horsfall, a large, dour man. He catches Midgley's eye and shakes his head in despair.

MIDGLEY I worry about Coretta's attention span, Mrs Azakwale.

Coretta is paying no attention at this moment, either.

It's very short.

MRS AZAKWALE I'm saying: she bin concentratin' on getting through puberty. Once that's out of the way I reckon it's all plain sailin'. (*moving away*) Now then, Coretta, pigeon, where's this Computer Sciences gentleman?

Camera follows Mrs Azakwale and Coretta as they go off, leaving Midgley facing Mr Horsfall and his son. The camera goes back to Midgley with Horsfall in full flow. His innocent-looking sports jacket notwithstanding, the boots, black trousers and blue shirt proclaim Mr Horsfall a policeman in mufti.

HORSFALL He's had every chance. Every chance in the world. Chance after chance after chance. I've lost count of the number of chances he's had.

MIDGLEY Martin is a little young for his age.

HORSFALL Martin? Is that what you call him?

MIDGLEY That's his name.

HORSFALL His name is Horsfall. Martin is what we call him, his mother and me. For your purposes I should have thought Horsfall was sufficient. Are you married?

MIDGLEY Yes.

HORSFALL And you teach him English? He can scarcely string
two words together. Why, Martin? Why? I can. Your father.
I have to. People making their statements, who is it who finds
them the right word? Me. At four o'clock in the morning after
a day spent combing copses and dragging ponds, making
house-to-house enquiries, I can do it. The father. But not the
son. Why? Say something, Martin.
Martin says nothing.
I mean: a school like this. Soccer facilities: tip-top. Swimming
bath: tip top. Gymnasium: tip-top. You want to be grateful.
We never had chances like that did we, Midgley?
Midgley, uncomfortable at finding himself handcuffed to Horsfall
in the same personal pronoun, says nothing. There is a pause.
Miss Tunstall comes up, anxious to attract Midgley's attention,
but sensing this is an awkward silence and therefore part of what
is being said, she waits a moment then makes little waving signs
behind Mr Horsfall's head; who, a policeman and ever alert to
mockery, turns round.

MISS TUNSTALL (*addressing Horsfall, not Midgley*) The hospital's
just rung. Mr Midgley's father's been taken ill. (*Only then does*
she look at Midgley.) Your father's been taken ill.

INT. SCHOOL OFFICE. DAY.
Midgley is on the telephone. Miss Tunstall is sitting at the desk, waiting
to start typing.

MIDGLEY They're ringing the ward. It's a stroke, apparently. And
he's had a fall.

MISS TUNSTALL You want to pray it's not his hip. That's
generally the weak spot. The pelvis heals in no time,
surprisingly. (*She doesn't sound surprised.*) Mother broke her
pelvis. I thought it was the beginning of the end.

MIDGLEY Hello?

MISS TUNSTALL She took a nasty tumble in Safeways last week.
They do when they get older. It's what you have to expect. I'm
reconciled to it now. Their bones get brittle.
She cracks her fingers and begins to type.

MIDGLEY No, I don't want Maintenance. I want Ward 7.

Miss Tunstall stops typing.

MISS TUNSTALL It's these ancillary workers. Holding the country to ransom. Other people's suffering is their bread and butter. (*She starts typing again softly.*)

MIDGLEY Midgley. Midgley.

She stops typing.

I'm his son. (*He waits.*) I see. Thank you. (*He puts the phone down.*) He's critical. They say it's touch and go.

MISS TUNSTALL How old is he?

MIDGLEY Seventy-two.

MISS TUNSTALL My mother's eighty-two. Life is unfair.

Midgley is still standing by the telephone when the headmaster breezes in.

HEADMASTER On the phone again, Midgley? I'm the one who has to go cap in hand to the Finance Committee.

MISS TUNSTALL Mr Midgley's father's ill. It's touch and go.

She starts typing like the wind.

INT. HEADMASTER'S STUDY. DAY.

HEADMASTER Of course you can go. Of course you must go. One's father. There can be no question. It's awkward of course. But then it always is. Was he getting on in years?

MIDGLEY Seventy-four.

HEADMASTER Seventy-four. Once upon a time I thought that was old. (*He looks at the timetable, a vast complicated affair.*) Let me see. It's English, Integrated Humanities and Creative Arts. Nothing else, is there?

MIDGLEY Environmental Studies.

The Headmaster groans.

HEADMASTER That's the bluebottle in the Vaseline. Pilbeam's away on a course. That's the trouble with the environment. It involves going on courses. I shall be glad when it's a proper subject and confined to the textbooks. Ah well. I have no parents. They were despatched years ago. A flying bomb.

The Headmaster makes this sound like a victory for common sense.

MIDGLEY He must have been lying there two days.

HEADMASTER A familiar scenario. Isolated within the community. Alone in the crowd. You must not feel guilty.

MIDGLEY I generally go over at weekends.

HEADMASTER It will give Tomlinson an opportunity to do some of his weird and wonderful permutations with the timetable. Though I fear this one will tax even Tomlinson's talents . . .
He has opened the door to let Midgley out. They go back into Miss Tunstall's office.

INT. SCHOOL OFFICE. DAY.

HEADMASTER . . . One must hope it is not as grave as it appears. One must hope he turns the corner. Corners seem to have gone out nowadays. In the old days the sick were always turning them. Illness now much more of a straight road. Why is that?

MIDGLEY Antibiotics?

HEADMASTER Ye–es. One has the impression modern medicine encourages patients to loiter. Mistakenly, one feels. God speed. (*He looks at the notice Miss Tunstall has been typing.*) Ah yes. Hooliganism in the swimming baths. (*He reads the notice.*) I'm not sure if we've couched this in strong enough terms, Daphne.

MISS TUNSTALL It's as you dictated it.

HEADMASTER I have no doubt. But I feel more strongly about it now. Nothing else is there, Midgley?
Midgley shakes his head, smiles weakly at Miss Tunstall and goes out.
A boy slips. Is pushed. We are talking about concussion. A broken neck. A fatality, Daphne. I intend to nail the culprits. I want them to know they will be crucified.

MISS TUNSTALL Shall I put that?
The Headmaster looks at her sharply.

HEADMASTER First this business of Midgley *père*. Ask Tomlinson to step over, will you? Tell him to bring his coloured pencils. And a rubber.

INT. MIDGLEY'S HOME. KITCHEN. DAY.
The same scene as the second shot. Midgley sat with his coat on at the kitchen table, carving knife in front of him, while his wife prepares his sandwiches.

MIDGLEY I have treated him so badly. All along.
Mrs Midgley says nothing, but grimly spreads the bread.

I wanted to go over this last weekend. It's my fault.

MRS MIDGLEY Tomato or my jam?

MIDGLEY Tomato. I just never expected it.

MRS MIDGLEY I did. Last time I went over he came to the door to wave me off. He's never done that before. I think people know. *Pause.*

MIDGLEY He does come to the door. He invariably comes to the door.

Mrs Midgley shakes her head sensitively.

MRS MIDGLEY He was trying to tell me something. I know a farewell when I see one. (*She puts the sandwiches, flask, in front of him and waits.*) Is there anything else you want?

INT. MIDGLEY'S HOUSE. SITTING ROOM. DAY.

Another part of the house. Mrs Midgley is seen first, so that we at first think Midgley has gone. She is dusting. Her mother is sat in a chair, asleep. She is an old lady. No reference is made to her.

MIDGLEY'S VOICE I'm not going to let him down. I want to be there when he goes. He loved me.

Mrs Midgley picks up an item and dusts beneath it, viciously.

Don't you think so?

He is stood in the doorway watching her.

MRS MIDGLEY I do. Though why, I can't imagine. It's not as if you take after him. (*She dusts something else, grimly.*) One little bit.

Mrs Midgley's mother wakes up.

MOTHER Is it Saturday today?

INT. MIDGLEY'S HOUSE. THE STAIRS. DAY.

Midgley is sat on the stairs. Mrs Midgley is out of shot, still ruthlessly cleaning.

MRS MIDGLEY'S VOICE He had strength. Our Colin is going to be strong. He loved Colin.

MIDGLEY Does he know?

MRS MIDGLEY Yes. It hasn't hit him yet. When it does he's going to be heartbroken. They both are. Poor old Frank. *Pause.*

MIDGLEY I've never understood why you call him Frank. He's my father.

MRS MIDGLEY He has a name. Frank is his name.

MIDGLEY You're the only one who uses it. Everybody else calls him Dad. Or Grandad.

MRS MIDGLEY I call him Frank because that's the name of a person. To me he is a person. That's why we get on.

Mrs Midgley's mother appears at the door of the sitting room.

MOTHER Joyce.

MIDGLEY Yes, Mother?

MOTHER When is that chiropodist coming?

MIDGLEY Yesterday, Mother. He came yesterday.

INT. MIDGLEY'S HOUSE. COLIN'S BEDROOM. DAY.

Loud music. The door opens. Midgley comes in and stands waiting. Colin, his teenage son, switches the music off.

COLIN Dad, I've told you before. Don't just walk in. Knock.

MIDGLEY I did knock.

COLIN This is my room. I could be doing anything.

MIDGLEY I've got to go over to Bradford. To the hospital. Grandad's poorly.

COLIN I know. Mum said. I thought you'd have gone by now. I'm really sorry.

Midgley closes the door and music starts again as he goes downstairs.

INT. MIDGLEY'S KITCHEN. DAY.

Joyce's mother sits on a kitchen chair throughout this.

MIDGLEY Why don't you come?

MRS MIDGLEY With Mother? How can I?

MIDGLEY Ta ra, then. (*He kisses her and goes to the back door and opens it, then stops.*) Anyway, it isn't.

MRS MIDGLEY It isn't what?

MIDGLEY It isn't why you get on: treating him like a person. You get on because you both despise me.

MRS MIDGLEY Your father is dying. A good, good man is dying. And you hang about here resenting the fact that he and I were friends. I seem to have married someone very low down in the evolutionary chain. You might want one or two tissues.

Mrs Midgley takes some tissues and stuffs them in his pocket.

MIDGLEY When you and he were together I didn't exist.

MRS MIDGLEY Your father is *dying*. Will you exist now?

MIDGLEY I'll make it right. I'll be there when he goes. I'll hold his hand. I shan't let him down. If I let him down now I'll never be able to make it right. He'd stay with me the rest of my life. I did love him, Joyce.

MRS MIDGLEY I would like him to stay with you for the rest of your life. I hope he does stay with you for the rest of your life. As an example. As somebody to live up to. I think of his kindness. His unselfishness. His unflagging courtesy. The only incredible thing is that someone so truly saintly should have produced such a pill of a son. But I suppose that's your mother.

MIDGLEY Shut up about my mother. My mother is dead.

MRS MIDGLEY So is he, virtually. Dawdling. *Go.*

MIDGLEY Then things will change, you'll see. I'll change. I'll be a different person. I can . . . go. Live. Start!

He kisses her quickly and goes out.

EXT. MIDGLEY'S HOUSE. DAY.
Midgley is about to get into his van when Mrs Midgley comes after him with his flask and sandwiches.

MRS MIDGLEY *Start?* You're thirty-nine!

MONTAGE. MIDGLEY DRIVING FROM HULL TO BRADFORD. DAY.
An old man waiting to cross at a zebra. As he goes across he holds up his hand to stop oncoming traffic. Halfway across he changes into Midgley's father. Thereafter Midgley sees his father at every turn. Midgley's father sitting on a seat. Midgley's father waiting at a bus stop. Then Midgley's mother and father, the father carrying the shopping bag.

INT. HOSPITAL. LONG CORRIDOR. DAY.
The same long corridor we saw at the start of the film. Midgley is walking down it with Aunty Kitty, a woman in her seventies, his father's sister.

AUNT KITTY I thought you'd have been here a bit since. I was here at three o'clock. You'll notice a big change. He's not like my brother. He's not the Frank I knew. I don't dislike this colour scheme. I always liked oatmeal. The doctor's black.

INT. INTENSIVE CARE. WAITING ROOM. DAY.

MIDGLEY Did he know you?

AUNT KITTY The nurse says he doesn't know anybody. The
Duchess of Kent opened this unit, apparently. The kidney
department's world-famous.

A nurse comes in and Midgley gets up.

This is my nephew, Mr Midgley's son. Your father's got a room
to himself, love.

NURSE They all do, at this stage.

INT. INTENSIVE CARE. FATHER'S ROOM. DAY.

*Single ward. Midgley's father is lying motionless with his eyes open.
Monitors etc. on his chest. A window cleaner is washing the windows,
but with professional discretion avoids his gaze.*

MIDGLEY Dad. Dad. It's me, Denis. I've come. I've come, Dad.
It's all right. (*He pulls his chair up to the bed and holds his father's
hand.*) I'm sorry, Dad.

A nurse looks in at the door.

NURSE Are you next of kin?

MIDGLEY Son.

NURSE Not too long.

Midgley waits, holding his father's hand. Aunty Kitty comes in.

AUNT KITTY I wonder where he is? What does that look on his
face mean?

MIDGLEY It means that he is dying, and it's my fault.

*A nurse comes and stands at the door and they go out to the waiting
room again.*

INT. WAITING ROOM. DAY.

AUNT KITTY It's just a case of waiting now. There's a lot of
waiting done in hospitals. Ninety per cent of it's waiting.
(*stroking the upholstery*) Would you call this chestnut or russet?
(*Pause.*) I always thought I'd be the one to go first. They've
never got to the bottom of my complaint. They lowered a
microscope down my throat. Nothing there. I even went on
this machine the Duke of Gloucester inaugurated. That drew a
blank as well. Mr Conway Lewis said they were baffled.

There should be comings and goings through this.

I asked the nurse, I said: 'Is he just unconscious or is he in a
coma?' She didn't know. They don't get the training now.

MIDGLEY Aunty.

Aunty Kitty stops.

What was my dad like?

AUNT KITTY He never had a wrong word for anybody, your dad. He'd do anybody a good turn. Shovel their snow. Fetch their coal in. He was a saint. (*Pause.*) You take after your mother more.

INT. WAITING ROOM. A LITTLE LATER. DAY.

MIDGLEY I feel I lack his sterling qualities. Grit. Patience. That willingness to shoulder other people's burdens. Virtues bred out of adversity.

AUNT KITTY I think you change when you go to university.

MIDGLEY Deprivation, for instance. I was never deprived, Aunty Kitty. That way he deprived me, do you see?

AUNT KITTY I should have gone to secondary school. I left school at thirteen, same as your dad. You wouldn't think they'd have curtains in a hospital, would you? You'd think it wouldn't be hygienic.

MIDGLEY I know I had it easier than my dad. But I was grateful. I didn't take it for granted. It's not particularly enjoyable, education.

AUNT KITTY You used to look bonny in your blazer.

MIDGLEY He gave me what he'd wanted. Why should that be enjoyable?

AUNT KITTY You ought to be ringing round. Telling Ernest, Hartley and Christine. Mark's just got his bronze medal.

MIDGLEY I'll wait and see the doctor first.

AUNT KITTY You'd have thought they'd have had all these complaints licked, what with these silicone chips. Somebody's got their priorities wrong. Then he's always been a right keen smoker, your dad. Now he's paying the price. (*Pause.*) Robert Donat had bronchitis.

Midgley puts his head in his hands. Aunty Kitty, indicating a woman in a corner:

AUNT KITTY Her hubby's on the critical list. Their eldest girl works for Johnson and Johnson. They'd just got back from Barbados.

The doctor comes into the waiting room. He is an Indian doctor.
Midgley is dozing.

Denis. It's Doctor.

DOCTOR (*looking at his clipboard*) Mr Midgley? Your father has had a stroke. How severe, it is hard to tell. However, when he was brought in he was also suffering from hypothermia. Our old enemy. He must have fallen and been lying there for two days at least.

MIDGLEY I generally go over at weekends.

DOCTOR Pneumonia has now set in. His heart is not strong. I do not think he will last the night.

He puts the clipboard under his arm, and we see there is nothing on it.

INT. HOSPITAL TELEPHONE AREA. DAY.

Telephone in hospital: helmet type. A young man on one telephone, a fat man waiting.

FAT MAN Only three phones and two of them duff. You wouldn't credit it. (*He is standing. Midgley is sitting.*) Say you were on standby for a transplant. It'd be all the same.

He jingles his coins. The young man puts his head outside the helmet.

YOUNG MAN I've got one or two calls to make.

FAT MAN Oh hell.

PASSING MAN There's a phone outside Physio. Try there.

FAT MAN I'll try there.

Midgley waits, watching the young man. The young man watches Midgley but does not see him, while the following conversations ensue.

YOUNG MAN Hello, Dorothy? Dorothy, you're a grandma! A grandma. Yes. Well, guess. (*Pause.*) No. Girl. Seven and a half pounds. At 5.35. Both doing well. I'm ringing everybody. Bye . . . *Grandma.*

Midgley half-rises, but the young man makes another call.

Hello, Neil. Hi. You're an uncle. Yes. Just now. 5.35. Well, guess. (*Pause.*) No, girl. *No.* It's what we really wanted. I'm over the moon. So tell Christine, she's an aunty and yes, a little cousin for Josephine. How's it feel to be an uncle? Bye.

Midgley gets up and stands but the young man, while looking at him, ignores him.

Betty? Congratulations. You're an aunty. I won't ask you to guess. It's a girl. Susan's over the moon. And I am. I'm just telephoning with the glad tidings. Bye, *Aunty!*

MIDGLEY Could I just make one call?

YOUNG MAN Won't it wait? I was here first. I'm a father.

MIDGLEY I'm a son. My father's dying.

YOUNG MAN There's no need to take that tone. (*He steps out of the helmet.*) You should have spoken up. There's a phone outside Physio. (*He waits while Midgley telephones.*)

MIDGLEY Uncle Ernest? Denis. Dad's been taken poorly. He's had a stroke. And a fall. And now he's got pneumonia.

The young man looks away, abashed.

Can you ring round, tell anybody who might want to come? The doctor says he won't last the night. I'm in a box. There are people waiting.

He puts the telephone down.

YOUNG MAN You never know. They can work miracles nowadays.

INT. OUTSIDE THE HOSPITAL LIFT. EARLY EVENING.

UNCLE ERNEST Did you ring our Hartley?

Midgley nods.

Tied up? Secretary, was it?

MIDGLEY He's coming as soon as he can get away.

UNCLE ERNEST Was he in a meeting? I'd like to know what they are, these meetings he's in, that he can't speak to his father. Who are they in these meetings? Don't they have fathers? I thought fathers were universal. Instead of which, I have to make an appointment. 'I'll just look at his book.' Sons, fathers, you shouldn't need appointments, you should get straight through. You weren't like that with your dad. Frank thought the world of you.

INT. A LARGE HOSPITAL LIFT. EVENING.

UNCLE ERNEST This is what I'd call an industrial lift. (*He taps the side of it with his boot.*) It's not an ordinary passenger lift, this. It's as big as our sitting room. It'd be a stroke. He's only seventy-two. I'm seventy-four.

The lift stops and a porter gets in with a trolley with a woman on it.
PORTER Is it working?
The little head closes its eyes.
We've just had a nice jab. Had a nice jab and we're going for a
ta-ta.
UNCLE ERNEST She'll be on five thousand a year, Hartley's
secretary. That's a starting salary these days.
PORTER Gangway.
He wheels his trolley out.

INT. HOSPITAL. LONG CORRIDOR. EVENING.
UNCLE ERNEST I came on the diesel. It's only one stop. I use
my railcard. I go all over. I went to York last week. Saw the
Railway Museum. There's stock in there I drove. Museum in
my own lifetime. Tell you one thing: I wouldn't like to have to
polish this floor. You still schoolteaching?
MIDGLEY Yes.
UNCLE ERNEST Pleased your dad, did that. No. I've been all over
since your Aunt Edith died. Take a flask. Sandwiches. I plan to
visit Barnard Castle next week. Weather permitting.

INT. OUTSIDE INTENSIVE CARE. EVENING.
Uncle Ernest pauses.
UNCLE ERNEST Is your Aunty Kitty here?
MIDGLEY Yes.
UNCLE ERNEST I thought she would be. Where no vultures fly. . . .

INT. WAITING ROOM. EVENING.
*Aunty Kitty sees them come in and, as if her grief were too great for
words, solemnly embraces her brother, shaking her head and dabbing
her nose.*
AUNT KITTY I always thought I'd be the first to go.
UNCLE ERNEST You still might. He's not dead yet.
AUNT KITTY Go in, Ernest. Go in.

INT. INTENSIVE CARE. FATHER'S ROOM. EVENING.
Father alone with his brother. Ernest stands. Then sits awkwardly.
UNCLE ERNEST This is summat fresh for you, Frank. (*Pause.*)
You were always such a bouncer. (*Pause. He gets up and looks at*

the scanner, then sits down again.) I went over to York last week. It's the first time I've been since we used to bike over when we were lads. It hasn't changed much. They haven't spoilt it like they have Leeds.

The nurse looks in, says nothing, and goes away.

Though there's one of these precincty things. (*Pause.*) I went on my railcard. It's still wicked. (*Pause.*) I'll say ta-ra then, butt. Ta ra.

He jogs his brother's foot in farewell, just as the nurse comes in and sees.

NURSE (*reprovingly*) He's very ill. And this is delicate equipment.

INT. HOSPITAL LIFT. EVENING.

Hartley, Uncle Ernest's son, Jean, his wife, and their two children, Mark and Elizabeth.

HARTLEY Now think on, the pair of you, don't be asking for this, that and the other in front of your grandad.

JEAN Are you listening, Mark? Your father's talking to you. We don't want him saying you're spoiled.

HARTLEY Though you are spoiled.

JEAN Whose fault is that?

The lift doors open and Mark nearly knocks down a nurse.

Mind that nurse, Mark. Sorry.

INT. HOSPITAL. LONG CORRIDOR. EVENING.

Uncle Ernest is coming down the corridor with Midgley.

HARTLEY Look out. Here's your grandad. Now then, Dad. Denis.

JEAN Grandad. (*She kisses him.*) Give your grandad a kiss, Elizabeth.

The little girl does so.

Mark.

MARK I don't kiss now.

JEAN You kiss your grandad.

The boy does so shamefacedly.

HARTLEY How is he?

UNCLE ERNEST Dying. Sinking fast.

HARTLEY Oh dear, oh dear, oh dear.

MIDGLEY They don't think he'll last the night.

JEAN How've you been keeping?

MIDGLEY Champion.

HARTLEY I had the receiver in my hand to give you a ring, yesterday, Dad, only a client came in.

UNCLE ERNEST That one of them new watches?

MARK Yes. (*He shows him it.*)

JEAN He had it to save up for. You had it to save up for, didn't you, Mark?

ELIZABETH He didn't.

UNCLE ERNEST I didn't have a watch till I was twenty-one. Course they're twenty-one at eighteen now, aren't they? *Pause.*

HARTLEY We'd better be getting along to the ward if it's that critical.

JEAN Shall we see you soon, Grandad?

UNCLE ERNEST I was thinking of going to Barnard Castle next week.

JEAN Whatever for?

UNCLE ERNEST I've never been.

HARTLEY Say goodbye then.

JEAN Kiss your grandad.
   The children kiss him again.

MIDGLEY I'll just see you to the lift.
   Hartley and Jean and their children go along the corridor.

JEAN I'll give you such a clatter when I get you home, young lady. He did save up.

ELIZABETH Only a week.

HARTLEY Now, when we get there we shan't have to go in all at once. It'll just be two at a time.

JEAN What's he doing going to Barnard Castle? He can't be short of money, taking himself off to Barnard Castle.

INT. INTENSIVE CARE. FATHER'S ROOM. EVENING.
Dad in bed, as before. Hartley and Mark come in.

HARTLEY Hello, Uncle. It's Hartley. There's Mark too. We're all here.
   They stand awkwardly waiting. Hartley's attention is increasingly caught by the television monitor. The boy goes on looking distastefully at the bed.

You see this screen, Mark? It's monitoring his heartbeats.

MARK (*witheringly*) I know, Dad.

HARTLEY I was only telling you. You want to learn, don't you?

MARK Dad. We made one of those at school. Is he going to die?

HARTLEY Well, I don't know. Why?

MARK Jill says that if we get the chance of seeing someone dead we ought to take it. Jill says death is a part of life.

HARTLEY Who's Jill?

MARK She takes us for Modern Studies.

INT. WAITING ROOM. EVENING.

ELIZABETH Are you crying, Mam?

JEAN Yes.

The little girl looks at her mother.

ELIZABETH There aren't any tears.

JEAN You can cry without tears.

ELIZABETH I can't. How do you do it, Mam?

JEAN I'll give you such a smack in a minute, your Uncle Denis's father is dying.

Elizabeth starts to cry.

JEAN There, love. It's all right. He doesn't feel it.

ELIZABETH I'm not crying because of him. I'm crying because of you.

INT. WAITING ROOM. EVENING.

Midgley, Hartley and an Indian father and son, who are sat in a corner. The father is weeping and hugging the child very tightly. The child peers under his father's arm at them.

HARTLEY I wouldn't have another Cortina. I used to swear by Cortinas.

Midgley looks at the Indian family.

You still got the VW?

Midgley nods.

I might go in for a Peugeot next. A 604. Buy British.

Jean and Elizabeth come in, having been to see Father.

JEAN (*mouths at Hartley*) How long are we stopping?

HARTLEY I think we ought to wait just a bit, don't you, darling?

JEAN Oh yes. Just in case.

HARTLEY He was a nice old chap.

Aunty Kitty comes in.

AUNT KITTY I just had one coffee and a Wagonwheel, and it was forty-five pence. And it's all supposed to be voluntary.

MARK There isn't a disco, is there?

JEAN Disco? Disco? This is a hospital.

Aunty Kitty looks shocked.

MARK Leisure facilities. Facilities for visitors. Killing time.

JEAN Listen. Your Uncle Denis's father is dying and you talk about discos.

MIDGLEY It's all right.

HARTLEY Here. (*handing him a pound*) Go get yourself a coffee.

Aunty Kitty closes her eyes in despair.

INT. LONG CORRIDOR. EVENING.

A woman on sticks painfully hobbling to a radiator. She looks out of the window, alone. She speaks to no one in particular.

WOMAN I do love chrysanths.

HARTLEY You want to make it plain at this stage you don't want him resuscitating.

Midgley, Hartley and his family are walking down the corridor.

JEAN That is if he doesn't want him resuscitating.

HARTLEY I wouldn't.

JEAN Denis might. You don't know.

Midgley looks as if he doesn't know either.

HARTLEY You often don't get the choice. They'll resuscitate anybody, given half a chance. You read about it. Shove them on these life-support machines. It's all to do with cost-effectiveness. They invest in this expensive equipment, and then of course they have to use it.

The woman looking out of the window watches them go.

INT. OUTSIDE HOSPITAL LIFT. EVENING.

JEAN Miracles do happen, of course. I was reading about these out-of-body experiences. Have you read about them, Denis? Out-of-body experiences. Where sick people float in the air above their own bodies. I think it won't be long before science will be coming round to an afterlife. Bye bye, love.

Shot of the whole of Hartley's family as the lift door closes.

INT. HOSPITAL. LONG CORRIDOR. EVENING.
Midgley goes down the corridor. The woman is still at the window.
WOMAN They've put me down for one of these electric chair
   things. Once I get one of them I shall be whizzing about all
   over.

INT. WAITING ROOM. EVENING.
The Indian father and son are both asleep. Aunty Kitty and Midgley
are the only other occupants of the waiting room.
AUNT KITTY Money's no good. Look at President Kennedy.
   They've been a tragic family. (*Pause.*) The Wainwrights got
   back from Corfu. They said they enjoyed it but they wouldn't
   go again. (*Pause.*) If I go now I can just get the twenty to.
MIDGLEY I'll come down and phone Joyce.
   Aunty Kitty looks at the sleeping Indians.
AUNT KITTY The little lad's bonny. They've got feelings the same
   as us. They're fond of their families.
   They are out into the corridor.
   More so probably, because they're less advanced than we are.

INT. HOSPITAL. TELEPHONE AREA. EVENING.
Midgley on the telephone.
MIDGLEY I've got to be here.

INT. MIDGLEY'S HOME. SITTING ROOM. EVENING.
Mrs Midgley's mother asleep. His son watching televison. Mrs Midgley
on the telephone.
MRS MIDGLEY You've done all that's necessary. Nobody would
   blame you.

INT. HOSPITAL. TELEPHONE AREA. EVENING.
MIDGLEY I've got to be here. I must be here when he goes. Can't
   you understand that?

INT. MIDGLEY'S HOME. SITTING ROOM. EVENING.
MRS MIDGLEY I understand you. It's not love. It's not affection.
   It's yourself.
   She puts the telephone down.

COLIN Dad?

MRS MIDGLEY He's hanging on.
  Pause.

COLIN Who?

MRS MIDGLEY Your *grandad.* Wake up, Mum. Time for bed.

INT. INTENSIVE CARE. FATHER'S ROOM. NIGHT.
*Midgley is sitting by the bed. We see the day nurse with her cloak on,
outside, and the night nurse taking over. The night nurse, Valery, comes
in and does jobs round the bed.*

MIDGLEY Am I in the way?

VALERY No. Stop there.
  *He watches her. She is less pert than the others, more sloppy. She
  smiles at him and goes out.*

INT. INTENSIVE CARE. FATHER'S ROOM. NIGHT. LATER.
Night nurse looks in.

VALERY Cup of tea?

INT. INTENSIVE CARE. NIGHT NURSE'S DESK. NIGHT.
Midgley is having his tea. She is working on various forms.

VALERY Slack tonight. Still, it just takes one drunken driver.
  Midgley is dropping asleep.
  I thought you were going to be a bit of company. You're tired
  out. Lie down.
  She gives him a pillow and they go out to the waiting room.

INT. WAITING ROOM. NIGHT.

VALERY I'll give you a shout if anything happens.
  The Indians are also asleep.

INT. INTENSIVE CARE. FATHER'S ROOM. NIGHT.
*Four in the morning. His father's screen regularly blipping. His father's
face.*

INT. WAITING ROOM. DAY. NEXT MORNING.
*Midgley is being shaken by the day nurse, as unsympathetic as the
night nurse had been the reverse.*

NURSE You can't lie down. You're not supposed to lie down.

Midgley sits up. The Indians have gone and in their place two anonymous people are staring at him expressionlessly.

MIDGLEY The nurse said she'd wake me up.

NURSE What nurse?

MIDGLEY If anything happened to my father.

NURSE Which is your father?

MIDGLEY Midgley.

NURSE Is that a hospital pillow?

MIDGLEY Mr Midgley.

NURSE No. No change. But don't lie down. It's not fair on other people.

INT. INTENSIVE CARE. FATHER'S ROOM. DAY.
Midgley and his father. Midgley looking rough and unshaven. His father pink and clean and fresh.

EXT. HOSPITAL. DAY.
Midgley walks round the hospital and goes to his van in the car park. He looks at himself in the car mirror, then gets out and walks round the outside of the hospital. It is a modern building, built in identical units, so that one ward looks much the same as another. A woman is stood at a window suckling a baby. He looks at her, then a nurse appears behind her and draws the blinds. Midgley walks on. He finds himself outside Intensive Care. He looks up at his father's room. There is a nurse stood with her back to the window. She moves back to allow someone else in. Midgley can see someone in a white coat, another nurse. The room seems full of people.
He begins to scramble down the bank to try to get into this section of the building. He tries a door: locked. He scrambles along the bank, round the outside of the building, tries another door. A man on a telephone sees him: puts the telephone down and picks up another. Midgley scrambles on, eventually finding himself in some bushes. He runs through the bushes, across a muddy flowerbed and finds himself at the main entrance.

INT. INTENSIVE CARE. FATHER'S ROOM. DAY.
Midgley rushes past the desk into his father's room.

MIDGLEY Is he dead?

The nurses look round.

MATRON Dead? Certainly not. I am the matron. Look at your shoes.

As the nurses bustle Midgley out he looks back and we get a glimpse of his father's face and he could be smiling.

MIDGLEY But I want to see a doctor.

MATRON Why? Have you a complaint?

MIDGLEY The doctor yesterday said my father wouldn't last the night. He has, so I was wondering if there was any change.

MATRON No change. I should go home. You've done your duty.

INT. WAITING ROOM. DAY.

Aunty Kitty has got her knitting, a flask, biscuits. She is quite settled in. The Indians are back waiting, too.

AUNT KITTY I've just been to spend a penny. When you consider it's a hospital, the toilets are nothing to write home about. (*She is immersed in* Country Life.) I wouldn't thank you for a house in Portugal. Loggia. Swimming pool. I just want somewhere I can get round nicely with the Hoover. Where've you been with your shoes?

Midgley looks at his muddy shoes.

You'd better ring your Uncle Ernest. He'll want the latest gen.

INT. HOSPITAL. GENTS' TOILET. DAY.

Midgley gets some toilet paper and cleans the mud off his boots. He has put his shoes on again and is standing with the muddy toilet paper in his hand when an orderly comes in, looks at him and the paper with incredulity and disgust, and goes into a cubicle shaking his head.

ORDERLY The bastard public. The nasty, dirty, bastard public.

Midgley looks at the paper and puts it in the bin.

INT. HOSPITAL. TELEPHONE AREA. DAY.

Midgley waiting. No sense of urgency. A woman is on the telephone.

WOMAN Cyril. It's Vi. Mam's had her op. Had it this morning, first thing. She's not come round yet but apparently she's fine. Yes, fine. I spoke to the sister, and she says it wasn't what they thought it was, so there's no need to worry. I don't know what it was, she did tell me the name, but the important thing is that it wasn't what they thought it was. No. Completely clear. The sister would know, wouldn't she? Oh yes, I think it's good

news, and she said the surgeon is the best. People pay thousands
to have him, she said. Anyway I'll see you later. I'm so relieved.
Aren't you? Yes. Bye.
Midgley goes to the telephone.

INT. INTENSIVE CARE. FATHER'S ROOM. DAY.
Uncle Ernest looking at him.
UNCLE ERNEST Jillo, Frank. We can't go on like this, you know.
  I can't run to the fares.

INT. WAITING ROOM. DAY.
Uncle Ernest and Hartley are leaving. Midgley with them.
AUNT KITTY It's Frank all over. Going down fighting. He loved
  life. He won't go without a struggle . . . It's their eldest
  daughter . . . (*She indicates an elderly couple waiting.*) Just
  choosing some new curtains in Schofields. Collapsed.
  Suspected brain haemorrhage. Their other son's a vet.

INT. HOSPITAL. LONG CORRIDOR. DAY.
UNCLE ERNEST It's a wonder to me how your Aunty Kitty's
  managed to escape strangulation so long. Was he coloured, this
  doctor?
MIDGLEY Who?
UNCLE ERNEST That said he was on his last legs.
MIDGLEY Yes.
UNCLE ERNEST That explains it.
HARTLEY Dad.
UNCLE ERNEST What do you mean 'Dad'?
HARTLEY I mean I'm vice-chairman of the Community Relations
  Council, that's what I mean. I mean we've got one in the office
  and he's a tip-top accountant. We all have to live with one
  another in this world.
UNCLE ERNEST You're young.

INT. OUTSIDE THE LIFT. DAY.
UNCLE ERNEST I'll not come again. Again and again. It gets
  morbid. I'd go back home if I were you.
  Midgley says nothing.

HARTLEY He's got to play it by ear.

UNCLE ERNEST There's no need to go through all this performance with me, you know. Come once, and have done. Mind you, I'll be lucky if you come at all.

The lift doors open.

HARTLEY Shall I drop you?

UNCLE ERNEST I don't want you to go out of your way.

HARTLEY No, but shall I drop you?

Midgley watches the doors close on them still arguing. It is like a play within a play of his relations with his own father.

INT. HOSPITAL. LONG CORRIDOR. DAY.

Midgley walks back.

WOMAN ON STICKS I'm getting one of these mobile trolley things. Once I get that I'll be up and down this corridor.

INT. INTENSIVE CARE. FATHER'S ROOM. NIGHT.

The night nurse (Valerie) comes in with a bowl and a sponge.

VALERY (*night nurse*) He doesn't want to leave us, does he?

As she washes his father's thighs Midgley gets up suddenly and stares out of the window.

I can see his attraction even though he's old. I can imagine women going for him.

Midgley isn't liking any of this.

MIDGLEY Women didn't go for him. Only my mother.

VALERY I don't believe that.

Midgley turns just as she is sponging between his father's legs. He turns away hastily.

What was he?

MIDGLEY How do you mean?

VALERY His job?

MIDGLEY Plumber.

VALERY What are you?

MIDGLEY Teacher.

VALERY He's got lovely hands. Real lady's hands. You see that happen in hospitals. People's hands change.

Midgley turns and she is holding his father's hand.

INT. INTENSIVE CARE. NIGHT NURSE'S DESK. NIGHT. LATER.

A VERY YOUNG DOCTOR There hasn't been any particular change. His condition certainly hasn't deteriorated. On the other hand it hasn't improved.

MIDGLEY The other doctor said he wouldn't last the night.

YOUNG DOCTOR I don't know there's any special point in waiting. You've done your duty.

MIDGLEY I don't think he is dying.

YOUNG DOCTOR Living, dying. (*Shrugs slightly.*) There's nothing special about the moment of death. The screen will alter, that's all. You do *want* your father to live, Mr Midgley?

MIDGLEY Yes, only I was told he wasn't going to last long.

YOUNG DOCTOR Our task is to make them last as long as possible. We've no obligation to get them off on time. This isn't British Rail.

MIDGLEY Look, how old are you?

The doctor turns away, pulls a small face at Valery, and goes.

INT. INTENSIVE CARE. NIGHT NURSE'S DESK. NIGHT. LATER.
She is being sympathetic.

MIDGLEY I don't like fifteen-year-old doctors, that's all. I'm old enough to be his father.

VALERY Why not go and sleep in your van? If anything happens I'll send somebody down.

MIDGLEY Does nobody else wait? Does nobody else feel like me? (*Pause.*) What do you do during the day, when you're on nights?

VALERY Sleep. I generally surface around three.

MIDGLEY Maybe we could have a coffee? If he's unchanged.

VALERY OK.

MIDGLEY I'll just have another squint, then I'll go. (*He goes into his father's room. Camera stays with her. Midgley returns, quickly.*) Come look. He's moved.

INT. INTENSIVE CARE. FATHER'S ROOM. NIGHT.
Valery goes briskly and professionally ahead of him into the room and looks at the old man.

VALERY No.

MIDGLEY Yes.
  She switches on the overhead light.
  He's kind of smiling.
VALERY No.
MIDGLEY If you look long enough you'll see a smile.
VALERY If you look long enough you'll see anything you want.
  You're tired. Goodnight.
  Midgley would probably kiss her, were his father not present.

INT. MIDGLEY'S HOME. NIGHT.
*Mrs Midgley on the telephone. Her mother sits with her bag by the
sitting-room door.*
MRS MIDGLEY Sit down a second, Mother. I'll be with you in a
  minute. Mum's waiting to go up. She's crying out for a bath.
  I'm just steeling myself. What do you do all day?

INT. HOSPITAL. TELEPHONE AREA. NIGHT. MIDGLEY ON THE
TELEPHONE.
MIDGLEY *I* need a bath.

INT. MIDGLEY'S HOME. NIGHT.
*Mrs Midgley watching her mother, whose handbag has slipped to the
floor; she is trying to retrieve it.*
MRS MIDGLEY Go over to your dad's. It's not all that far. If it's
  not going to be any minute, you might as well. I'm going to
  have to go.
  Her mother nearly falls off the chair, but she stops her in time.
MOTHER What am I doing sitting on this chair? I never sit on this
  chair. I don't think I've ever sat on this chair before.

INT. HOSPITAL. LONG CORRIDOR. NIGHT.
*Midgley in the long corridor. The Matron comes down the corridor on
her electric trolley, a vision like the first appearance of Omar Sharif out
of the heat haze in* Lawrence of Arabia. *Midgley watches.*

EXT. CAR PARK. MORNING.
Nurse Lightfoot (Valery) is banging on the window.
VALERY (*mouthing*) Just coming off.

Midgley winds the window down.
Isn't it a grand morning? I'm just coming off. I'm going to
have a big fatty breakfast then go to bed. I'll see you at
tea-time. You look terrible.
*Midgley sees his face in the driving mirror. He does. She walks off
and he starts up the van and drives after her.*
MIDGLEY I forget to ask you. How's my dad?
VALERY No change. (*She waves and runs down towards the nurses'
flats.*) No change.

EXT. STREET IN LEEDS. DAY.
A terrace house. Midgley's van outside.

INT. FATHER'S HOUSE. DAY.
*Midgley in his father's house: neat, silent. Photographs of father and
mother. A wedding. Photographs of grandchildren.*

INT. FATHER'S SCULLERY. DAY.
*Midgley pours water from kettle into a bowl. He looks at his father's
razor. Cleans it. Changes the blade. Finds his father's old shaving
brush, worn down to a stub. Uses ordinary soap. Wipes his face on the
towel on the back of the door. Takes his shirt off. Washes. Smells his
shirt. Goes upstairs.*

INT. PARENTS' BEDROOM. DAY.
*Neat: dressing table set with glass dressing-table set, mirror and brush
etc. Looks in drawer. Finds a new shirt, still in Christmas paper. Puts it
on. Too big. Looks at socks. Underpants.*

INT. FATHER'S SITTING ROOM. DAY.
*Midgley, dressed, downstairs standing in front of the fireplace. He looks
as if he's ready for a funeral. His father's pipe is on the mantelpiece.
He looks at it. Puts it back. It falls to the hearth. He stoops to pick it
up, then suddenly thinks of his father doing the same, falling and lying
there.*

EXT. FATHER'S HOUSE. DAY.
*Midgley then panics, thinking of his father dead, and rushes out of the
house and drives away very quickly.*

INT. CORRIDOR IN HOSPITAL. DAY.
Midgley running down it.

INT. CORRIDOR. INTENSIVE CARE. DAY.
A trolley being wheeled out, body sheeted. Midgley stops and it passes.
It is followed by the Indian father and son.
AUNT KITTY I offered them my condolences but I don't think
    they understood.

INT. INTENSIVE CARE. FATHER'S ROOM. DAY.
MIDGLEY I'm wearing your shirt, Dad. It's the one we gave you
    for Christmas. I hope that's all right. It doesn't really suit me
    but I think that's why Joyce bought it. She said it didn't suit
    me so it would suit you.
    The day nurse comes in. She raises her eyebrows, indicating she
    thinks he is mad, talking. Midgley coughs.
    They tell you to talk. I read it in *Reader's Digest*. It was in the
    waiting room.
NURSE They say the same thing about plants. I think it's got past
    that stage.

INT. NURSES' HOME. VALERY'S ROOM. DAY.
They have just had tea.
VALERY People are funny about nurses. Men. You say you're a
    nurse, and their whole attitude changes. Do you know what
    I mean?
MIDGLEY No.
VALERY I've noticed it at parties. They ask you what you do, you
    say you're a nurse, and next minute they're behaving like
    animals. Perfectly ordinary people. They turn into wild beasts.
    I've given up saying I'm a nurse for that reason.
MIDGLEY What do you say you are, medieval historian?
VALERY No. I say I'm a librarian. But that's why I liked you.
    You're obviously not like that.
    Midgley is silent.
    Of course, you've got other things on your mind.
MIDGLEY What?
VALERY He is lovely. Your dad. I do understand the way you feel
    about him. Old people have their own particular attraction
    I think. He does, anyway.

Midgley is restive.

Was your cake gritty?

MIDGLEY No.

VALERY Mine was. Mine was a bit gritty.

MIDGLEY It was probably meant to be gritty.

VALERY No. It was more gritty than that.

Silence.

MIDGLEY What would you say if I asked you to go to bed?

VALERY I suppose it's with you being a nurse: they think you've
seen everything. When? Now?

MIDGLEY Yes.

VALERY I can't now.

MIDGLEY Why not? You're not on till seven.

VALERY No. It's Wednesday. I'm on early turn.

MIDGLEY Tomorrow, then.

VALERY Tomorrow would be better. Though of course it all
depends.

MIDGLEY What on?

VALERY Your father. He may not be here tomorrow.

MIDGLEY No. I'd better go back then.

VALERY Fingers crossed.

INT. INTENSIVE CARE. FATHER'S ROOM. DAY.

Dad unconscious still, Midgley whispering in his ear.

MIDGLEY Hold on, Dad. Hold on.

INT. HOSPITAL. TELEPHONE AREA. DAY.

MIDGLEY Colin. It's Dad. Is your mam there?

INT. MIDGLEY'S HOME. DAY.

COLIN She's upstairs with Gran. Mum. Dad wants you.

MRS MIDGLEY (*shouting*) I can't. I'm bathing your grandma.
I can't leave her.

COLIN She says she can't leave her.

INT. HOSPITAL. TELEPHONE AREA. DAY.

MIDGLEY You go up and watch her. I want to speak to your
mam.

INT. MIDGLEY'S HOME. DAY.

COLIN Dad, she's in the bath. She's no clothes on. Dad, I won't.
Mrs Midgley puts her head round the bathroom door.

MRS MIDGLEY Tell him if I can get a granny-sitter I'm going to come over.

COLIN She says she's going to come over.

INT. HOSPITAL. TELEPHONE AREA. DAY.

MIDGLEY (*alarmed*) No. Don't do that. Tell her not to do that.
There's no need. Are you there? Go on, tell her.

INT. MIDGLEY'S HOME. DAY.

COLIN I'll tell her.

INT. HOSPITAL. TELEPHONE AREA. DAY.

MIDGLEY You won't. You'll forget. Go up and tell her now.
Midgley waits.

INT. MIDGLEY'S HOME. DAY.

COLIN Mum. Dad says there's no need.

MRS MIDGLEY No need to what?

COLIN Go over.

INT. HOSPITAL. TELEPHONE AREA. DAY.

MIDGLEY Did you tell her? Good. Haven't you forgotten something? 'How's Grandad, Dad? Is he any better?' 'Nice of you to ask, Colin. He's about the same, thank you.'

INT. MIDGLEY'S HOME. DAY.

Colin putting the telephone down wearily, as Mrs Midgley comes in with a wet towel and a bundle of underclothes.

MRS MIDGLEY How was your grandad?

COLIN About the same.

MRS MIDGLEY And your dad?

COLIN No change.

EXT. HOSPITAL CAR PARK. THE VAN. DAY.

Bright sunshine. Midgley asleep. Someone gets into the van.

MIDGLEY Who's that?

HIS FATHER Only me.

MIDGLEY Hello, Dad.

FATHER I thought we'd go for a drive.

They drive off.

MIDGLEY When did you learn to drive?

FATHER Just before I died.

MIDGLEY I never knew that.

FATHER There's lots of things you don't know.

EXT. MONTAGE. DAY.

They are driving along. The scene should change dramatically and inexplicably. Country. Town. Back streets.

FATHER Isn't that your mam when she was younger? (*He stops the van and a pretty woman gets in.*) Mam.

MOTHER Hello, Dad. Hello, Denis. What a spanking van.

FATHER Move over, Denis.

Midgley is suddenly a small boy.

Let your mam sit next to me.

They sit in a line and Midgley sees his dad's hand on his mother's knee.

EXT. A FIELD. DAY.

Midgley, as a boy, is sitting with his mother in a field.

MOTHER This field is spotless. It's a lovely field. We can sit here all day. Just the two of us.

Midgley, as a boy, has turned round, and on the edge of the field, unseen by his mother, is a huge slag heap. He is horrified.

Aren't you glad we brought a flask?

A man is running down the slag heap. The boy is frightened. The man runs through the grass. He is covered in grime. It is his father. His mother is in white.

BOY Mam. Mam.

She looks round.

MOTHER It's only your dad, love.

She smiles and he sits down beside her, his black hand on her white frock.

INT. LEEDS MARKET. DAY.

Then Midgley and his mother and father, now old, are walking through Leeds market, the place empty, the stalls shuttered and closed.

218

EXT. MOTORWAY. DAY.
The van is driving along a motorway. The turn-offs are marked with the names of places like Leeds, Barnsley, Sheffield. Then they change to Heart Disease, Cancer.

INT. HOSPITAL RECEPTION. STATION. DAY.
His father is sitting down and he is in the reception area of the hospital, but it is also some kind of station. His mother sits beside him. They kiss, and look round, but Midgley is not there.
Above their heads there is a station noticeboard, but instead of Arrivals and Departures it is marked 'Births and Deaths' and keeps clicking over with different names. She kisses his father goodbye and goes through the gates, just as Midgley comes up. He shakes the gates shouting 'Mam, Mam.' But she has gone. He turns round and looks at his father who is shaking his head. He is disappointed with him. Midgley shakes the gates again, calling 'Mam, Mam' as it changes to Valery knocking on the window of the van to wake him.

EXT. HOSPITAL. CAR PARK. DAY.
He sits up. Valery is tapping on the window. She waves and goes off towards her quarters. Midgley sits thinking.

EXT. HOSPITAL. CAR PARK. DAY.
It is later on that day, and the car park is more full. A smart car draws up, driven by a woman. She gets out. She is elegantly dressed, and is in her late fifties or early sixties. She walks towards the hospital.

INT. FATHER'S ROOM. INTENSIVE CARE. DAY.
Midgley comes into his father's room. The woman is sitting there, holding his father's hand. She is unruffled.
ALICE Is it Denis?
MIDGLEY Yes.
ALICE I'm Alice Duckworth. Did he tell you about me?
MIDGLEY No.
ALICE No. He wouldn't, the old bugger. He told me about you.
  Never stopped telling me about you. It's a sad sight. Though
  that slut of a nurse says he's a bit better this morning. His
  condition's stabilised, whatever that means. Shouldn't think
  she knows. You look a bit scruffy. I've come from Southport.

(*She gets up and puts the carnations in the bin.*) Carnations are depressing flowers. (*She replaces them with flowers she has brought herself.*) I'm a widow. A rich widow. Shall we have a meander round? No sense in stopping here. His Lordship's not got much to contribute.

Alice and Midgley go out through the waiting room.

INT. WAITING ROOM. DAY.
Aunty Kitty begins to get up, but Mrs Duckworth walks straight past her. Aunty Kitty follows them out.

INT. LONG CORRIDOR. DAY.
Into the corridor. Mrs Duckworth is walking briskly off, followed by Midgley.
ALICE That your Aunty Kitty?
  Midgley nods.
  I thought so.

INT. RECEPTION AREA. DAY.
They are having coffee. Alice taking out a flask from her bag.
ALICE Do you want a drop of this in it?
MIDGLEY No thanks.
ALICE I'd better, I've driven from Southport. I wanted to marry your dad, did you know that? He said no. Why? Because I'd got too much money. My husband left me very nicely placed; he was a leading light in the soft-furnishing trade. Your dad would have felt beholden, you see. That was your dad all over. Couldn't bear to be under an obligation. Still, you know what he was like.
MIDGLEY He was good. Everybody says how good he was.
ALICE He always had to be the one, did Frank. The one who did the good turns, the one who paid out, the one who sacrificed. You couldn't do anything for him. I had all this money, he wouldn't even let me take him to Scarborough. We used to go sit in Roundhay Park. Roundhay Park! We could have been in Tenerife. (*She blows her nose.*) Still, I'd have put up with that.
MIDGLEY That's why I've been waiting. That's why I wanted to be here. I didn't want to let him down. And he wants me to let him down, I know.

INT. HOSPITAL. LONG CORRIDOR. DAY.

ALICE What was your mam like?

MIDGLEY She was lovely.

ALICE She must have had him taped. She looks a grand woman.
He's showed me photographs. (*She makes herself up.*) Anyroads.
I'll go and have another look at him. Then I've got to get over
to a Round Table in Harrogate. Killed two birds with one stone
for me, has this trip.

MIDGLEY You don't know. If he comes round he might
reconsider your offer.

She looks at Midgley and smiles, then gives him a kiss.

ALICE And don't you be like your dad, think on. You go your
own way.

INT. WAITING ROOM. INTENSIVE CARE. DAY.

AUNT KITTY Your mother'd not been dead a year. I was shocked.

MIDGLEY I'm not shocked.

AUNT KITTY You're a man. It wasn't like your dad. She's got
a cheek showing her face.

MIDGLEY I'm rather pleased.

AUNT KITTY And her hair's dyed. A real common woman.
Anyway they're sending him downstairs tomorrow. He must be
on the mend. I'll not stop much longer. I hope when he does
come round he's not a vegetable. Where are you going?

MIDGLEY I said I'd see someone.

*Aunty Kitty is left in the waiting room. A woman comes in from the
ward.*

AUNT KITTY How's your hubby? Still in a coma? (*She shakes her
head in mute sympathy.*) There must be a purpose somewhere.
(*She pops a toffee in her mouth.*)

INT. VALERY'S ROOM. DAY.

Midgley is brushing his teeth, out of the room.

VALERY Maureen knows to ring if anything happens. Not that it
will. His chest is better. His heart is better. He's simply
unconscious now. I'm looking forward to him coming round.
I long to know what his voice is like.

INT. VALERY'S BATHROOM. DAY.

Midgley in the bathroom. Midgley turns the tap off.

MIDGLEY What?

VALERY I long to know what his voice is like?

MIDGLEY Oh. Yes. (*He turns the tap on again.*)

INT. VALERY'S ROOM. DAY.

VALERY I think I know. I'd just like to have it confirmed.

> *Midgley comes in.*

> You don't like talking about your father, do you? (*She is undressing.*) Nice shirt.

MIDGLEY Yes. One of Dad's.

VALERY Nice.

> *He goes to the bathroom and we see her take the telephone off the hook. Midgley gets into bed. She is already in bed.*

MIDGLEY Hello. (*Pause.*) It's a bit daft is this.

VALERY Why? It happens all the time.

MIDGLEY It's what people call living, is this. We're living.

> *They kiss.*

> I ought to have done more of this.

VALERY What?

MIDGLEY Living. This is going to be the rule from now on. I've got a lot of catching up to do. This, it's the thin end of the wedge.

VALERY I've never heard it called that before.

MIDGLEY Dirty bugger.

VALERY You started it. 'What would you say if I said could we go to bed.' I mean.

MIDGLEY That's technique, that is. It avoids direct confrontation.

VALERY I think I could do with some confrontation.

MIDGLEY You've done this before. Hey, stop. I hope this isn't one of those private beds. It's not BUPA is it, this? Otherwise I may have to leave. I'm opposed to that on principle.

VALERY People do talk rubbish in bed.

MIDGLEY Only place left. Only place where you can act daft. Not that we do. Mrs Midgley and me. If Joyce ever does anything fresh I know it's because she's been listening to some rubbish on *Woman's Hour.*

VALERY You never asked me if I was married.

MIDGLEY You're a nurse. You're above marriage. (*Pause.*) Are
  you married?
VALERY He's on an oil rig.
MIDGLEY I bloody hope so.
  Midgley takes off his glasses and the scene fades out.

THE SAME. LATER.
MIDGLEY I feel better after that, Nurse.
  Valery lights a cigarette.
  Can I have one of those?
VALERY You don't smoke.
MIDGLEY I don't do this, either. (*He lights a cigarette.*) I'm in bed
  in the afternoon, smoking a cigarette with another woman,
  post-coitally. (*Pause.*) I was certain they were going to ring.
VALERY No.
  *She smiles, shows him the receiver is off, and puts it back on. He
  frowns, then smiles.*
MIDGLEY That was a risk. Still, we are now going to be taking
  risks. The new, risky life of D. Midgley. Do you think I ought
  to be getting back?
VALERY We've still got half an hour.
MIDGLEY Hey, you're insatiable, you.
VALERY I know.
  *They put out their cigarettes and are just settling down again when
  the telephone rings.*
VALERY Yes? Yes. (*She is looking at Midgley as she is speaking.*)
  You'd better go.
MIDGLEY What's matter?
VALERY Go.
MIDGLEY Had she been trying before?
VALERY You'd better go.
MIDGLEY (*frantic*) Had she been trying?
VALERY Go.
MIDGLEY Where's my glasses?

INT. HOSPITAL. THE CORRIDOR. DAY.
  Doors burst open and Midgley runs down.

INT. INTENSIVE CARE. FATHER'S ROOM. DAY.
Aunty Kitty, Mrs Midgley, Midgley.

AUNT KITTY It's the biggest wonder I hadn't popped in to see
    Mrs Tunnicliffe. She's over in Ward Seven having a plastic hip
    – she's been waiting two years – but, I don't know what it was,
    something made me come back upstairs and I was sat looking
    at some reading matter when in walks Joyce, and we'd hardly
    had time to say hello when the nurse comes running out to say
    he had his eyes open. So we were both there, weren't we, Joyce?

MRS MIDGLEY He just said, 'Is our Denis here?'

AUNT KITTY And I said, 'He's coming, Frank. It's me, Kitty.'
    And he just smiled a little smile and it was all over. It was a
    beautiful way to go. I'm glad I was here to see it. I was his only
    sister. (*Pause.*) The dots do something different when you're
    dying. I wasn't watching it, naturally, but out of the corner of
    my eye I noticed it was doing something different during his
    last moments.

MRS MIDGLEY He's smiling.
    *The body lies on the bed, sheet up to the neck. Midgley goes to the
    window.*

MIDGLEY Of course he's smiling. He's won. He's scored. In the
    last minute of extra time.
    *Mrs Midgley looks disgusted. Porters appear to transfer the body on
    to a trolley. Mrs Midgley goes out.*

AUNT KITTY It's a pity you weren't here, Denis. You've been here
    all the time he was dying. What were you doing?

MIDGLEY Living.

EXT. FATHER'S ROOM. INTENSIVE CARE. DAY.
They are coming out. Valery is there. Midgley looks, but says nothing.

AUNT KITTY He just said 'Is our Denis here?' then smiled that
    little smile, and it was all over.

INT. HOSPITAL OFFICE. DAY.
*A counter. Hospital administrator, going through a form. Dad's folded
clothes on the counter.*

HOSPITAL ADMINISTRATOR One gunmetal watch. Wallet with
    senior citizen's bus pass. Seventy-four and a half pence in
    change. One door key.

He pushes the form over for Midgley to sign.

MIDGLEY Have you something I can put them in?

HOSPITAL ADMINISTRATOR They never bring bags. It's not our
    job, you know, bags.
    *In the wallet there is a photograph of Midgley and his mother, when
    younger, stood together laughing. He looks at this while the man
    roots about for a bag.*

INT. MIDGLEY'S HOME. KITCHEN. NIGHT.
*Midgley sat at the kitchen table. Mrs Midgley sat at the table. Both
still in overcoats.*

MRS MIDGLEY You didn't let him down. You went for a walk.
    That's not letting him down.

MIDGLEY I wasn't there.
    Colin comes in with a girlfriend.

COLIN Hello, Dad. Long time no see.
    Midgley doesn't respond.
    Did Grandad die?

MRS MIDGLEY This afternoon.

COLIN Oh. Jane's just going to have some coffee.

MRS MIDGLEY Take her in the other room.
    They go out. She calls.
    Put the fire on.
    She pours out the coffee.

INT. MIDGLEY'S HOME. HALL. NIGHT.
*Midgley goes out of the kitchen and is about to go upstairs when he sees
the sitting-room door ajar. He pushes it open. Colin is kissing the girl.
He watches for a second.*

MIDGLEY We've just lost your grandad. You might show some
    feeling.
    Mrs Midgley appears behind him with the coffee as Midgley goes.

MRS MIDGLEY Take no notice. He's upset. There's nothing to
    be ashamed of. It's only your father. (*She smiles sweetly.*)

INT. MIDGLEY'S SCHOOL. MISS TUNSTALL'S OFFICE. DAY.
Miss Tunstall is typing.

MISS TUNSTALL Well, at least he didn't suffer.

MIDGLEY Oh no.

She stops typing and reaches for her cigarettes.

MISS TUNSTALL When my mother finally pulls her socks up and dies I'm going to go on a world cruise.

MIDGLEY (*reaching for a cigarette*) May I?

MISS TUNSTALL I didn't know you smoked.

MIDGLEY I thought I might start.

MISS TUNSTALL Bit late in the day.

MIDGLEY What's this? (*He reaches over and takes the notice she is copying.*)

MISS TUNSTALL It's one of his 'privilege not a right' notices.

MIDGLEY (*reading*) 'Pupils are reminded that coming to school in their own cars is a privilege, not a right. There have been several unsavoury incidents recently . . .' I like 'unsavoury' . . . 'of pupils resorting to their cars in the lunch hour to indulge in sexual intercourse.'

Miss Tunstall hurriedly retrieves the notice to check this is just Midgley's joke.

MISS TUNSTALL 'Immoral behaviour.'

MIDGLEY 'Immoral behaviour.' Where are you going to go on this world cruise?

Miss Tunstall shrugs and starts typing again.

MISS TUNSTALL Bridlington, I expect.

INT. MIDGLEY'S SCHOOL. LONG CORRIDOR. LATE AFTERNOON.
Midgley walks down the long corridor. He is in his overcoat and carrying his briefcase. A small boy is looking out of the window. Midgley walks on down the corridor.

INT. HOSPITAL. LONG CORRIDOR. NIGHT.
The double doors and long corridor at the hospital, the credits over.